*I Want
My Life
Back!*

Also by Lorraine Bossé-Smith (with John Jackson)

Leveraging Your Communication Style

Leveraging Your Leadership Style

Leveraging Your Leadership Style Workbook

I Want My Life Back!

Life Management for Busy Women

LORRAINE BOSSÉ-SMITH

Abingdon Press / Nashville

This book is printed on acid-free paper.

Library of Congress Cataloging-in-Publication Data

Bossé-Smith, Lorraine, 1966–
    I want my life back : life management for busy women / Lorraine Bossé-Smith.
        p. cm.
    Includes bibliographical references.
    ISBN 978-0-687-49278-7 (binding: adhesive perfect : alk. paper)
    1. Time management.   2. Stress management for women.   I. Title.

    BF637.T5B67 2008
    248.8′43—dc22

2008019135

Scripture taken from the Holy Bible, NEW INTERNATIONAL VERSION®. Copyright © 1973, 1978, 1984 by International Bible Society. All rights reserved throughout the world. Used by permission of International Bible Society.

"Make It a Habit" by Lorraine Bossé-Smith on page 84 is copyright © 2004 by Lorraine Bossé-Smith.

As with any exercise or weight loss program, you should consult a health care professional before starting any new physical activity or weight loss/management program. Neither the author nor the publisher assumes any responsibility for incidents that may arise from following the advice provided.

08 09 10 11 12 13 14 15 16 17—10 9 8 7 6 5 4 3 2 1

MANUFACTURED IN THE UNITED STATES OF AMERICA

To my friends Virginia and Karolyn

*You don't know each other, but you have both become friends
that I never imagined I would have, enriching
my life beyond words.
Thank you for loving me as I am yet bringing out my softer,
more feminine, more fun self.
I couldn't have written this book without you in my life,
encouraging me always to work on balance.
I love you.*

Contents

Contents

Part Three: It's Time to Take Charge!

Acknowledgments

God has certainly answered my prayers! I have dreamed of writing more books, and here I am. Thank you, Lord!

With the help of friends and colleagues, we are getting out messages near and dear to my heart. Bless you!

I have many cheerleaders and supporters I am grateful for, but I particularly want to thank Mary and Delana for their prayers and encouragement. I look forward to our lunches!

As always, my husband is my biggest fan, and I love him for it! Thank you, Steve, for your hard work in helping me make dreams come true.

Introduction

How Did I Get Here and When Did I Become My Mother?

When in the world are we going to begin to live as if we understood that this is life? This is our time, our day...and it is passing. What are we waiting for?

—RICHARD L. EVANS

 "I'll start exercising when the kids are older."

"I'll start concentrating on me after work slows down."

"I've just got too much on my plate."

"I just need to get past this busy season."

The list goes on. As a personal trainer and life coach, I have heard countless statements from people, especially women, that lead me to believe we really don't understand that this *is* our life, and we do not get a second chance.

Perhaps you have caught yourself making one of these statements. I completely understand; in fact, I've made them myself. It simply means you are human! But you can do something about it, which is why I'm glad that you have picked up this book!

Life is much more complicated than in years gone by, and as women, we have double the workload. I recently attended a workshop where we were asked to name the different "hats" we wear on a given day. As I started labeling my hats, I realized that women really are expected to be many things to many people. Here is what my list looks like:

- Wife
- Child of God
- Friend
- Sister
- Daughter-in-law
- Pet owner
- Business owner
- Personal trainer
- Fitness instructor
- Life coach
- Mentor
- Executive coach
- Facilitator
- Author
- Trainer
- Speaker
- Leader

I might be missing a hat or two, but even so, it's certainly a big list—even overwhelming. Why don't you make your own list?

_____

_____

_____

_____

_____

_____

_____

_____

_____

_____

I am sure your list will be just as long, if not longer, especially if you have children. The list will give you a good idea of the many different directions you are being pulled in and the amount of energy you are expending. I know that you are stressed out and feeling the ramifications of wearing many hats. Statistics tell us we all are.

Totally Out of Control

The National Mental Health Association reports that 75 to 95 percent of all visits to the doctor are stress-related. Over half the population is overweight, and 80 percent of us suffer from back pain. One million Americans have heart attacks each year, and eight million have stomach ulcers (*A Healthier, Happier You,* pp. 10-11). Stress can also cause: low energy, restless nights and lack of sleep, digestive problems, memory impairment, depression or anxiety, decreased productivity, unhappiness, frequent illness, low sex drive, and serious illness.

Are you experiencing any of these symptoms? Stress may be to blame. Even if your stress is work-related, it can negatively affect your personal life, and vice versa. Unfortunately, our best attempts to compartmentalize our stress don't really work; stress *will* follow us. Marital problems, financial worries, even your troubled teens will come to work with you. Similarly, pressing deadlines, a mean boss, and uncooperative coworkers will come home with you at the end of the day. It's no wonder we don't feel good! Here's a fact, ladies: if we aren't doing something with our stress, it is doing something to us. We cannot passively sit by and let stress destroy our lives. We need to get our lives back!

Most folks are about as happy as they make up their minds to be.
—ABRAHAM LINCOLN

I was asked to speak to a group of Girl Scouts on the topic of stress. When I asked the girls, ages ten to twelve, to define stress for me, one girl replied, "It's a headache." Another girl offered, "It's a stomachache." Then a girl in the back yelled, "It's when I kick the dog!" Even our children understand what stress feels like! But what exactly is it?

What Exactly Is Stress?

Stress is a small word that packs a powerful punch! Personally, I believe it is responsible for most ailments, fatigue, missed deadlines, and dissatisfaction in our lives. Stress, in a nutshell, is a chemical reaction to the wear and tear on your body caused by life's events. Our adrenal glands are pumping, our blood pressure is elevated, and our cortisol levels have increased. Cortisol is a stress hormone that increases sugar (glucose) in the bloodstream and alters our immune system response. You've heard the expression "fight or flight"? It refers to our body's ability to shift into high gear in times of trouble. It was useful in prehistoric times when we needed to run away from a wild animal, but it can cause problems in our civilized world. With the pace of life we are living now, our bodies are constantly trying to run away. We may not have wild animals chasing us, but stress is around every corner. People, events, and media messages bombard us. Sometimes we may feel that we are on a treadmill with the speed stuck on high! Help!

Unhappiness is not knowing what we want and killing ourselves to get it.

—DON HEROLD

Different Types of Stress

In order to better understand stress, I like to break it down into three types: negative stress, positive stress, and motivating stress.

We are quite familiar with *negative stress*. We feel it during difficult times of life, such as when we experience death, divorce, or the loss of a job. During such times, we know we are under duress and can feel the effects physically, mentally, emotionally, and spiritually.

What some of us don't realize is that we experience stress even in the happy times of life, such as getting married, having a baby, or moving into a new house. Although these are wonderful moments, they come with what I call *positive stress*. Anyone who has planned a wedding understands this all too well. It is the most exciting time of your life, and yet you are stressed out by the endless details and family dynamics. The pressure is on for you to make this the most spectacular event. That is what I call stress! Here's the kicker: our bodies do not distinguish between the two; the same chemical reaction takes place.

> *Whether feeling negative or positive stress, our body's chemical reaction is the same.*

Last is *motivating stress,* which allows us to get to work on time, meet deadlines, and get things done. I also use the term *life pressures.* Time clocks, calendars, schedules, to-do lists—they all serve a purpose for us, but they create some stress. Without them, however, we wouldn't function nearly as efficiently, and that would cause another kind of stress altogether. As a writer, I am given a deadline for my manuscript along with guidelines regarding the book's length. Motivating stress helps me complete it on time and as promised. Could I write without a due date? Yes, but having the pressures keeps me on target and helps prevent procrastination. We all need those little nudges in life.

Are you a runner? I took up running about ten years ago, but I'm certainly not a die-hard runner—those folks who run at a good clip for ten miles at a pop. I'm more into three-to-five-mile runs at a leisurely pace. Nevertheless, one day I was out running at warp speed. I amazed myself, actually. I was breaking every record I had for that particular loop. I even began thinking of signing up for a marathon—*until* I turned around. It was then that I realized I had been running *with* the wind (positive stress). Once I had to run against the wind, I could barely move (negative stress). My motivating stress became: *Just get home!* Stress is in every aspect of our lives.

No Such Thing as Stress-free

As much as we would like to believe commercials, ads, and promises for a life of complete peace and tranquility, we will never live a life with zero stress. But somehow, we do need to realize that today is the only day of its kind we will experience. Tomorrow is already in the past. We do not have the opportunity to relive it. What happened or didn't happen is already a memory. We need to concentrate on the here and now. Unfortunately, as a society we have fallen into the trap of virtually sleepwalking through our lives. Then we wake up some morning wondering, "What in the world happened to me?" I hear it from women every day.

It Sneaks Up on Us

A client came in to see me for an assessment of her physical condition. On the telephone, she mentioned that she might be a few pounds overweight. When she came to my studio, she told me that she had gotten out of the habit of exercising. Her work schedule was extremely busy, and before she knew it, her life got out of balance. She was spending most of her time at work and very little time on things she enjoyed.

I always like to set benchmarks for my clients, so we measured her and determined her body fat percentage. When I reviewed the numbers with her, she turned white and began to cry. She was confronted finally with reality: she was obese. She was eighty pounds overweight, with over fifty percent of her body consisting of fat—the red zone for heart disease and other ailments. All she could say was, "How did this happen?" Well, days had turned into weeks, months, and eventually years. Now she found herself in a place she didn't like and she had to get herself out. The good news is that she took the first step, and we began to look at how she was handling stress.

You need to do the same thing. And like my client, you'll find that taking small steps *will* make a huge difference.

Don't forget until too late that the business of life is not business, but living.

—B. C. FORBES

Stress Reactions

I don't know about you, but my parents never told me about any of this. I had to figure it out on my own. As a result, most of us end up with our own ways of dealing with stress. Some of us work our way through it, while others drink ourselves numb. The unhealthy ways of dealing with stress seem easy to find:

- Overeating
- Undereating
- Alcoholism
- Misuse of legal and illegal drugs
- Smoking
- Emotional outbursts
- Control issues
- Anger
- "Workaholism"

How are you currently managing your stress? Is it working? Think of others you encounter in your life; how are they coping? The other day I ran to the office supply store. Two registers were open, and one had no line. The other register had a customer ringing up and a lady waiting. Since the lady was there first, I asked, "Do you want to check out at the other register since no one is waiting?" She proceeded to bite my head off, barking, "I will check out wherever I like, and you have to wait on my decision!" OK! I guess I was the straw that broke her back. I proceeded to check out at the other register.

As a society, we are wound up way too tight and are living on the edge. That's the reason for this book: to help you take steps in all areas of your life to bring balance—to regain your life, one piece at a time! In order to do that, we must be honest with ourselves. How did we end up here? What is stress costing us?

Turning Points

For me, it was a major crisis that forced me to evaluate my life. I had just turned thirty and had been transferred to England with my then-husband, who was in the Air Force. I was in an abusive marriage but had chosen to suffer silently. You know: "I made my bed, and now I need to sleep in it." That was how I was raised.

Besides the ongoing stress of our relationship, I had the stress of leaving my family and friends and quitting my own career to make the move. I did what I always do to cope: I got involved, figuring that if I stayed busy, I wouldn't have time to think. If I didn't have time to think, then I couldn't feel anything. And if I couldn't feel anything, I wouldn't hurt. Ever think that way? Stinking thinking!

Anyway, I volunteered at the church, taught fitness classes, and began substitute teaching in the American schools. I felt I was doing OK, until my mother came to visit for Christmas. When she got off the plane, she didn't know who I was—and half her face was paralyzed. My world came to a screeching halt. She was quickly diagnosed with an inoperable, terminal brain tumor. I needed to get her back to the States...and with that, my husband threatened to divorce me. If I left to help her, he would leave me. That was my defining moment. I left England and never went back.

In five short months I watched my mother die before my eyes. She and I had had our problems, but I loved her deeply. During that same time period, I went through a painful divorce. However, I was expending so much energy to love my mother through her last days that none of that mattered. What I didn't realize is that I wasn't managing all of the stress well at all. Finally, one day shortly after my mother's funeral, I could barely get out of bed. I had dropped down to ninety-seven pounds (at nearly five feet, ten inches tall). I had lost so much muscle that my body could barely function; it had started to shut down. That was my turning point. I knew I had to learn how to manage stress better, or it truly would kill me.

I needed to get my life back.

The Silent Killer

You may be hurting. You may be exhausted, overwhelmed, and feeling completely out of control. You may doubt whether you can ever get your life back, but I am here to tell you that you can! You can overcome your challenges, big or small, and create a healthier life for yourself and your loved ones. I encourage you to commit to changing your life, step by step. In this book I will try to help you with ideas, tips, and suggestions, so you don't feel like the woman who left this note:

> *If I'm not here, I'm lost.*
> *I've gone to look for myself.*
> *If I should return before I get back,*
> *Please have me wait until I return.*
>
> —ANONYMOUS

Ten short years after my turning point, I took a cruise with my new husband, who truly is a gift from God, to celebrate my big 4-0 birthday. As I reflected on all that had transpired in my life, I was extremely grateful that I learned healthier ways to manage my stress. It did not kill me, and with God's help I had survived and conquered! I had rebuilt my career, created a happier marriage, and restored my body by exercising and eating right. God truly had blessed me and continues to bless me. Friends, there is life beyond stress! Don't lose hope . . . ever.

Trust in the LORD with all your heart
and lean not on your own understanding;
in all your ways acknowledge him,
and he will make your paths straight.
—PROVERBS 3:5 NIV

Reflection

Something about turning forty made me look more closely at myself. Even though I had come a long way, I started evaluating how I approached life. Maybe it meant I was finally growing out of some old habits and beginning to mature and develop new ones.

Perhaps you have felt the same thing. Have you ever looked in the mirror and seen your mother? Yikes! When did that happen? I worked so hard not to become like her. I love my mother and miss her terribly, but I had been trying not to follow in her footsteps. As I have grown older, though, I've started to see my mother's strengths. She was a fighter, a trooper, a hard worker, and she was honest and dependable. She loved her family more than anything in the world. OK, I find that I inherited her critical eye for dust and like to keep a clean house. I am particular and like things a certain way. I could have inherited worse qualities. Certainly if I focus hard enough, I can see some of her not-so-flattering traits in myself, but those are places where I choose to grow and learn. For the most part, turning forty has helped me appreciate the good things I received from both of my parents. My parents made mistakes. They can't undo them, and neither can I. What I can do is love, forgive, learn, and move on to a new and improved me.

A New You

Whether you feel that turning into your mother is a good thing or a scary thing, you have the opportunity to be your own person. You can choose the traits you wish to keep and toss the ones that do not serve you well. Life is nothing more than choices we make...and then living with those choices. The awesome thing about God is that even if we make a horrible decision, he stands by us. And his will *will* be done!

You may have had a painful divorce like me or some other hardship. Whatever you have struggled with, what do you want your tomorrow to look like? Let us not focus on what we have lost but rather on what we can gain.

> *Let us not focus on what we have lost*
> *but rather on what we can gain.*

As a fitness professional, I have learned one thing: it is never too late to get healthy! Even when we mistreat our bodies for years, if we get serious about doing the right things, the body will respond. So it is with you and a better life: it is never too late to reduce your stress and improve the quality of your life. That is my mission. In fact, that is why I get out of bed every day. Whether I am speaking, training, teaching, or writing, I want to improve the quality of *your* life. And that is why I have written this book.

I want to share with you what I have learned through my trials and ordeals. I want to encourage you to believe that better days are ahead and you will get there! Together we will look at your life and help you make improvements to bring balance back to your world.

I'm so glad that I've been able to change. I relax more, laugh often, listen to my body, and give it what it needs. I am human, though, and am painfully aware that managing stress is an everyday thing. We will never "arrive," but we can enjoy the journey a lot more.

So, what do you say? Are you ready to say goodbye to your hectic, harried life and hello to a happier and healthier one? Let's create a new you, together. I consider it an honor to walk with you in the pages that follow.

Are you ready to get *your* life back? Let's go!

Part One

It's Time
to Manage!

1.

So Much to Do,
So Little Time

Time is the scarcest resource and unless it is managed, nothing else can be managed.

—PETER DRUCKER

 Ticktock. Ticktock. Time is certainly ticking away. Wherever you are, a clock is clicking away the minutes. Another one just went by as you read this sentence. Time waits for no man (or woman) and keeps marching on. In order to help you get some of your life back, we must look at how you manage your time. Are you organized? Do you keep a tidy house, everything in its place? Are you a master of scheduling and planning? Or are you like many women I know: constantly running late, forgetting appointments, never quite getting to everything you need to do and feeling frustrated?

Many clients have come to me in sheer desperation, their lives utterly out of control and their stress levels at the max. Unfortunately, a lifetime of hearing people say, "Do what feels good; I'm OK, you're OK" deceived us into believing that we didn't have to do certain hard things like manage our time. One client rebelled against my suggestions, saying they would confine her, restrict her creativity, and make her unhappy. Well, she was already miserable; what did she have to lose? The reality of getting your life organized is that you *will* have more free time and less stress. This, in turn, will allow you to have extra creativity and joy. Interested?

It Takes Commitment

Let me ask you this before we go any further: What would you do with an extra thirty minutes? I actually want you write it down here, so please take a moment to think about it and respond.

_____

_____

_____

_____

_____

_____

_____

No answer is wrong. This is *your* extra thirty minutes. Would you sleep? Exercise? Play with the kids? Visit family? Work? Read? By managing your time better, you can easily gain thirty minutes every day! Use what you wrote as motivation to apply the principles in this book.

Want to get really serious? Then fill in and sign the success contract below. I have every coaching and fitness client sign one. Although the contract is not legally binding, it puts on paper your commitment and your promise to do the work. If you want to get the most out of this book, I encourage you to fill this out and have a loved one or trusted friend sign as your accountability partner. I'll be your coach!

Success Contract

I, _____, hereby make a commitment to read this book with the intent of changing my time management, thoughts, emotions, physical condition, relationships, and spiritual life. I do want my life back!

I agree to try and apply the principles, tips, and suggestions in this book for at least thirty days.

When I have kept this agreement, I believe and trust that I will be a healthier and happier person. I will celebrate by

_____

_____

_____

Signature: _____

Date: _____

Witness: _____

Date: _____

I always include a place to spell out what you will do when you succeed, because I firmly believe that we need to celebrate our victories! Too often, especially in the workplace, we move from one goal or achievement to the next without pausing long enough to say, "Good job" or "Well done!" I won't lie to you; getting your life back will take some work because it took a while to get out of balance. The good news is that it won't take nearly as long to get it back into shape.

One of the most surprising things for clients who come to me to lose weight is how quickly they can get to a healthy weight. Oftentimes, years and years of doing the wrong things and not doing the right things gets a person overweight. But in a matter of months, a person can get to a good weight. That's encouraging news, and so it is with your life. You will see improvements right away; it won't take you years to get more balanced, I promise.

It is no use saying, "We are doing our best." You have got to succeed in doing what is necessary.
—Sir Winston Churchill

Event Management

This chapter is going to help you manage your time, although that is a misnomer of sorts because we really can't control time at all. Time is what it is. Days are twenty-four hours long, weeks have seven days, and the months turn into years whether we like it or not. No matter what we do, we cannot slow down or speed up time.

What we can do, however, is control the events in our lives; and, after all, that's what life really is, a series of events. If we desire greater control and security, more order and less stress, then we must manage the events that make up our lives. In this book, therefore, when we refer to or discuss time management, we are in essence addressing event management.

You don't get to choose how you're going to die ... or when. You can only decide how you're going to live.
—Joan Baez

The pages that follow describe time- and event-management techniques that can dramatically improve the quality of your life by helping you regain some control, order, and peace. By managing some of the stuff of our lives better, we can enjoy our lives more fully. As you read through, you may find that some of the tips and suggestions are habits for you already. Bravo! Others may be new to you, and I encourage you to give them a try.

If you do what you've always done, you'll get what you've always gotten.

—ANONYMOUS

The First Step

When you read the introduction, did you list all the hats you wear? Were you surprised at how much you have going on? Like me, you probably had been aware that you were busy but didn't realize how many different ways you were expending energy. Each of our hats has a multitude of events associated with it. When I coach people on managing their time and events more efficiently, one of the first things we do is to list those events and look at the cost associated with each of them. We know what we pay for gas and a gallon of milk, but most of us really don't have a clue about how much we pay for the events in our lives.

All events are not created equal. For instance, you will expend much more energy doing something you really don't want to do compared with something you enjoy. We'll address setting boundaries in the next chapter, but for now let's just say that without setting limits, you won't be in control.

Be deliberate with your life. Too often, we think that we have to say yes to everything. We feel obligated. We must change that mind-set to one of evaluating what we do and determining what *we* see fit to do. I call it the Opportunity Scale.

29

The Opportunity Scale

Let me ask you this: As you are reading this book, what are you *not* doing? Some answers might be: not doing the laundry, not sleeping, not working, not feeding the dog. The truth is that as you read this book, you aren't doing *anything* else! By choosing to read it, you put a greater value on it at this moment than anything else. Thank you! I know you won't regret it if you stick with me.

On any given day or moment, opportunities present themselves to us. We have the choice to participate or not. And too often, my friend, that is what we have given up—our right to choose! Somewhere along the way, we just went along with life. Maybe as women we feel it is our duty. Well, ladies, it's time to get in the driver's seat!

> *Live as you will wish to have lived when you are dying.*
> —Christian Furchtegot Gellert

Think of opportunity in terms of a scale. When a choice comes along, weigh it against its cost.

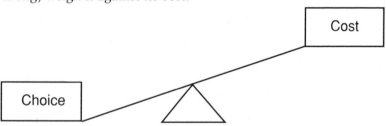

If the cost isn't too great, then you've made the right choice. If, on the other hand, the cost is too heavy, then you may want to reevaluate your decision. No right or wrong answers exist. I cannot tell you what to do, but I can tell you this: if you start being more consciously involved in your decision-making process, you will have less stress. As much as possible, make sure each opportunity outweighs the cost. This simple step will make a world of difference in your life. Start applying it immediately, OK?

The Secrets of Super-productive People

Now, back to those folks I briefly mentioned in the introduction, the ones you hate because they get everything done on time, are extremely organized, and seem to have it all together. What makes them so productive? Don't hate them; emulate them! You too can have a more organized life by using a system called IPPA. My husband and I developed it years ago, and ever since it has been helping folks get a handle on their lives. It is quite simple, really. IPPA stands for:

Identify what needs to be done.
Prioritize your goals and tasks in the order of their importance.
Plan when and how your goals and tasks will be achieved.
Act to achieve them!

In order for the system to work, you must pause long enough to look at the tasks and events in your life and determine what needs to be accomplished. Once you've done that, you can prioritize the items, then plan and take action! Everyone is unique, so your process for doing this may be different from someone else's. Here's a selection of methods; see what works best for you.

- To-do list—A sheet of paper with your tasks listed. Down and dirty. Not fancy or formal.
- Planning sheet—Sheet of paper in a day planner that outlines your tasks and gives you ways of prioritizing them.
- Electronic device—PDA, cell phone, wireless handheld device, or other device that provides a means to keep your lists with you at all times.
- Sticky notes—Help you remember things on the fly.
- Goal list—A more formalized plan with specific details and due dates.
- Tickler file—A folder holding your to-do items in some order for you to retrieve.

- Calendar—A wall, pocket, or year-at-a-glance calendar offers daily and monthly tracking of events.
- Whiteboard—Write down or erase your to-do list as needed and keep it someplace visible.
- Other

I don't want you to get caught up in the how of doing it, as long as you accomplish the what. The one method I would highly discourage you from using, though, is the pile and bulldoze method. This consists of stacking up piles until you can't find anything and then giving up, ultimately tossing everything and starting over. Some argue from among the piles that they know exactly where everything is, but I say hogwash! Folks, it has been proven over and over again that when the world around us is cluttered, so are our minds. And when our minds are cluttered, so is our soul. To reduce stress and regain some sanity, we need order. It will take some work, but you can do it!

No Pain, No Gain?

As a fitness instructor and personal trainer, I tell people that I don't always agree with the saying "no pain, no gain." Exercising is work, but it shouldn't hurt to the point of your being unable to move! In the case of creating some order, though, depending upon who you are, you can expect a little pain.

> *When patterns are broken, new worlds emerge.*
> —TULI KUPFERBERG

For some people, managing tasks comes easy. They can't help it; it comes naturally. I know plenty of women who do not share that gift and they constantly struggle to stay afloat. If you are in the latter category, be encouraged. Anything done over and over again will get easier with time. When it comes to managing events, remember:

Keep it simple.
Be consistent.
Customize your plans to work for you.

The ABCs of Prioritization

An important part of the IPPA system is prioritizing what needs to be done in your life. Don't forget to use the Opportunity Scale here and evaluate the cost. Be very sure that you are willing to pay the price before you commit to doing something.

My friend Jim Canfield has a way of prioritizing, using the ABCs:

✦	A items are "alligators" and will bite you in the butt if you don't give them attention *now*. These are truly urgent and very important issues. Delay at your own peril.
✦	B things are "bears" that are hibernating right now, but when they awake, they might eat you! These are important but not urgent. Be sure to address them when necessary, or they will ruin your day.
✦	C matters are "crows." They may be loud and obnoxious because they sound urgent, but they aren't very important. Don't fall prey to their call.
✦	D issues are plain "dogs." Oh, they may be cute, but they are not urgent or important. Be careful about spending time here, or your peace of mind may go to the dogs.

(Jim Canfield, Executive Forums, 2007)

Whether you use Jim's method or your own, prioritize what matters most to you! One way to do this is to create a chart such as the one below, in which A, B, C, and D items are listed in the four quadrants, according to priority.

A / Alligators Urgent/Important	**B / Bears** Not Urgent/Important
C / Crows Not Important/Urgent	**D / Dogs** Not Important/Not Urgent

The D quadrant is probably where we lose the most time and receive the least back. These are trivial activities such as handling junk mail, forwarding e-mail, and engaging in idle chitchat that gobble up our time. Before you know it, you have wasted half your day. The Internet has really become a time waster. Couple that with television, and we don't have enough hours in the day to get everything done. Well, we would have time if we managed these tasks a little better. Monitor them carefully. I had a client who got sucked into surfing the web five or six hours a day. She had to set an alarm in order to stop and get on to what really mattered. Granted, you may find these activities relaxing, but keep it in moderation, especially if you feel you just don't have enough hours in the day.

Last, items in the C quadrant can also tie us up. Examples are talking on the telephone, chatting with a visitor, and other unexpected activities that are in your face but not necessarily important. By learning how to keep these brief, you can move on to what you need to do. I estimate that for every interruption you have while working on a project, you will need at least ten minutes to get refocused.

One of my clients decided to take the priority chart to heart and he drew it on the big whiteboard in his office. Every morning, he would write out his tasks and assignments in the appropriate space. Over time, he had less and less in the crisis quadrant and more in the planning one. His stress went down and his productivity went up!

There can be no happiness if the things we believe in are different from the things we do.

—FREYA STARK

It Is T.I.M.E.

If you haven't reflected lately on what matters to you, I suggest you give it some consideration. You would think we all know exactly what we want, but we don't. I love the scene in the movie *Bruce Almighty* when Bruce, played by Jim Carey, gets in trouble because he gave all the people on his prayer list what they wanted. He wreaked havoc, and millions of people won the lottery! God, played by Morgan Freeman, asks Bruce, "Since when do people know what they want?" Thankfully, in real life God doesn't give us everything we ask for, but we should have some sense of what is important to us.

To help my clients decide what they want, I suggest that they look at it using the framework of T.I.M.E.

Tasks we need to accomplish
Interests we enjoy
Money matters
Energy

We are constantly balancing these four areas. Where are you spending most of your time? Do you focus mostly on work or career? Do you spend enough time with family, friends, and God? Are you stressing over money? Are you planning for your future, or carrying a lot of debt? Is your life energizing you, or are you being drained by it? The answers to these questions can be telling. If you feel one area is being slighted, start spending more time in it. Planning can help you do the other stuff more quickly so you have the time available for what matters to *you*.

Planning Power

For every minute you spend planning, you will reap ten times the benefit! Planning provides clarity and concrete steps to ensure that the proper action will be taken. It can literally shorten the time it takes to get something done. What was it that you wanted to do with that extra thirty minutes? Planning will definitely give you more time to do it.

After you have identified and prioritized your tasks, be sure to add twenty percent to the time you think the tasks will take. And allow what I call *buffer spaces*. When we pack our schedule so tightly that we do not have room for error, we've created a disaster waiting to happen. Murphy's Law tells us that what can go wrong, will go wrong! So, allow some space in between appointments. If you don't need it, fine! You can do some planning or maybe just enjoy the break.

*Add twenty percent to your estimated time
and always have buffer spaces in your schedule.*

Personally, I plan using a combination of computer and hard copy. I enter my schedule and tasks into an electronic calendar and print out daily and weekly sheets. This way, if I am in my office, I use my computer. But when I leave for appointments, I carry the sheets with me. Others prefer PDAs, handheld wireless devices, or other high-tech stuff. One client uses a three-ring binder. She hole-punches important papers and to-do lists and places them in the binder. This way, everything is in one place. It works for her. Figure out what works for you, then use it.

Again, some folks rebel against getting this organized, saying it's not in their nature. Well, if you truly want more peace in your life, you will need to make some changes. Just remember that doing what you have been doing got you to a place you didn't like. If you want to be someplace else, you *will* need to do things differently.

I love the story of the man who walks to work every day. One day he falls into a gigantic pothole. He never saw it coming. He has to climb out and is filthy as a result. But he goes on his way. The next day, the man takes the exact same route and falls into the same pothole. He climbs out a little quicker this time but is still very dirty. The third day, he takes the same route but tries to step around the pothole. But alas, he still falls in and has to climb out. The fourth and fifth day, he takes the same route, falls in, and climbs out. That night, he tells his wife about the pothole and how he keeps falling in. Her response: "Take a different route to work!"

Chunk It Down

As you plan your tasks, don't try to take everything on all at once. This is a big mistake many people make. In fitness, it is the people who haven't exercised in five years. They go to the gym early in the morning and work out for four hours! After a few days, they are utterly exhausted and give up. They went too hard, too fast. Be cautious not to do the same thing with your projects, tasks, or events. If you have a major project to do at home, chunk it down into bite-size pieces.

How do you eat an elephant? One bite at a time!

Time Out

No, I don't mean taking a time-out, although if you have been really bad and feel you deserve one, I'll wait! What I am referring to here is the practice of assigning due dates for projects. It's amazing how many people skip over this important step.

As you set due dates, be sure to allow enough time for each stage. I know I am constantly amazed at how long it takes to do relatively simple things, such making a doctor's appointment. (I end up on hold for fifteen minutes.) If I don't allow enough time to complete the task, then I fall behind—unless I scheduled some buffer time. As a way to help you consider all the steps, try the method I call RTP, to help you consider resources, time, and people.

RESOURCES	TIME	PEOPLE
What items will you need in order to do the project? Do you have them on hand, or will you have to buy them?	How much time will be required for each phase? Overestimate to allow for the un-expected delay.	Whose help will you need? Who is involved with the project? Who is respon-sible? Who is di-rectly affected?

(*Mastering Time Management*, Concept One, Inc. page 50)

Be N.E.A.T.

To save time with paperwork, mail, and e-mail, I've developed a method that I call N.E.A.T.:

Needs action now! Urgent and important, so take care of it today.

Essential. Urgent but not important, so keep it handy.

Arrange it in a file. It is not urgent but may be important for future reference.

Toss it now, not later! It is neither urgent nor important. Get rid of it.

· Take Inventory

In California, we have fires and earthquakes to contend with. My husband and I recently evaluated our evacuation plans, putting things in strategic places in case we needed to leave in a hurry, God forbid. As I went through the house, I started taking inventory of what we had and what I couldn't live without. This drill made me consider what was really important, and, of course, I realized I had been there before. During my divorce in 1997, I learned that all I really needed was my toothbrush, some clothes on my back, and my Bible. Everything else was just stuff. Granted, I really enjoy the extras of life, but I realize I don't need as much as I sometimes think.

I pray you never experience a tragic event or natural disaster, but I would encourage you to take inventory of your life. The more you have, the more work will be involved. For each item, ask some questions:

- Do you need it to survive?
- Do you need it for financial purposes?
- Is it required by law?
- Does it have extreme personal value to you?
- Is it irreplaceable?

A friend of mine realized that he didn't like owning a home. He hated the work involved with it and felt trapped and tied down to it. So he bought a condo instead. He is much happier. Somewhere along the way, he had bought the house simply because it was the natural next step. Who says it has to be that way? Don't let society tell you what the American dream is—make your own! You will be much happier and less stressed!

Don't take anyone else's definition of success as your own. This is easier said than done!

—Jacqueline Briskin

Get Out of That Time Trap

Unlike my friend, I do enjoy owning a home. Gardening and cleaning the house are therapeutic to me. But everyone is different. And because of that, we each have certain time traps that we can fall into and get stuck in. As I share in my workbook *Overcoming Time Traps,* "a time trap is an event or attitude that can slow or even stop our productivity or forward momentum in achieving our goals. By recognizing, avoiding, or overcoming time traps, we can dramatically increase our success potential in all aspects of our life" (Concept One, Inc., p. 1).

Two types of time traps exist: internal and external. Internal traps are those we impose on ourselves, and the biggest of these is procrastination. Procrastination is probably the most common trap of all and is responsible for more disappointment, failure, and lost opportunities than all the other traps combined. Why, then, do we do it? People will often avoid something that they associate pain with. Unfortunately, not taking action will only make matters worse and increase the pain. Remember the Opportunity Scale? Using it is very helpful for folks who tend to procrastinate. Another effective technique is to do the hard stuff first and get it over with. Don't try to take too much on at once; chunk down your unpleasant task into manageable steps.

External traps are those that are imposed on us. Some examples involve interruptions, waiting, and technology. Below are brief descriptions and some strategies to help you with these traps. When you can, take a different route!

TIME TRAP	DESCRIPTION	SOLUTION
Interruptions	Telephone, mail, visitors, meetings, and distractions	Set specific times to make phone calls. Let calls go to voice mail when possible. Keep your door shut. Ask visitors if they can come back or meet you later when it is more convenient. Make sure meetings are necessary, and stay on point.
Waiting	On people, on ideas, on materials, on input, or for direction.	Have agreed-upon deadlines and follow up ahead of time. Be proactive and get what you can as early as possible. Obtaining half of what you were promised is better than nothing. Document the deadlines and copy those involved so no miscommunication can occur.

TIME TRAP	DESCRIPTION	SOLUTION
Technology	Internet, email, cell phones, computers, voice mail, and the like were created to serve us; instead, we have become slaves to them.	Get back in the driver's seat! Use these devices as they were intended but don't allow them to control your life. Turn off the cell phone. Set times for Internet and e-mail. When you can, communicate in person.

I could write an entire book just on time traps. Be honest with yourself as to where you are getting sucked in and losing valuable energy and time. We've discussed a lot of principles. Use what works and also try some new things. By managing your time and events more effectively, you will truly see improvements in your life.

Moving Forward

The time is now for you to do this. You have reached a critical place and you can't go backwards. You must move forward if you wish to have a better future. I'm here to coach you, and don't forget to ask for God's help. I know that some of this can be overwhelming to you, so don't take it all on at once and don't do it alone.

2.

I'm Not as Think as You Stressed I Am!

Death is not the greatest loss in life. The greatest loss is what dies inside of us while we live.

—DR. NORMAN COUSINS

 The pace of life is moving along faster and faster. Almost everything can now be obtained through a drive-through window, including alcohol and prescription drugs! We are constantly bombarded by noise and media messages; even our cell phones get spam. The only time we slow down is when we sleep, but even then some choose to "power sleep." Just reading that probably makes your heart race; I know typing it does for me! Here are some telltale signs that you are stressed to the max:

- You say "What's *your* problem?" several times a day
- You call every "how is my driving" bumper sticker that you see
- You frequently get the urge to strangle someone
- You offer people "air refills" for their heads
- You are sure that everyone has conspired to really tick you off
- You took a hot bath to de-stress and haven't come out in weeks!

All this madness has to stop or we are going to drop dead—literally! We are seeing more and more illness, and I believe stress is the culprit. It's one of the reasons I mentioned stress so prominently in the introduction to this book. Whether we are struggling with time or event management or with emotional challenges, we *will* feel stressed. I wanted you to begin thinking about stress before we tackled it here; oftentimes we must understand our pain before we can prepare ourselves to fight it.

However, in this chapter I don't want to focus on the negative consequences of stress. You aren't where you want to be and you know it. I want this chapter to be encouraging and inspiring for you. The last thing you need when feeling stress is more stress! So I am going to suggest a number of ways for you to manage your stress better. The suggestions may not be new to you, but my prayer is that I will be presenting them to you in a way that will make a positive impact. And I believe you are ready for a change; otherwise you wouldn't be reading this book.

> *Our dilemma is that we hate change and love it at the same time;*
> *what we want is for things to remain the same but get better.*
> —SYDNEY HARRIS

Again, try some things and see what works best for you. Personally, I love a hot bath. Typically, no problem is so big that I can't soak it away. My all-time favorite greeting card is one that says on the outside: "When I'm stressed, I take a nice, hot bubble bath." The inside message reads: "I've been in here since last Thursday!"

Keep Your Sense of Humor

Our mothers were right: laughter *is* the best medicine! Usually, though, our sense of humor is the first thing that goes when we are under pressure. In the classic movie *Mary Poppins,* one of my favorite scenes is when Uncle Albert, played by Ed Wynn, sings, "I love to laugh, loud and long and clear." You can't watch that part of the movie without starting to laugh yourself, because laughing is contagious! So laugh! Watch funny movies, read funny books, tell funny stories, and laugh at life. Laughing brings more oxygen to your body and gets your blood flowing. Try it. You can't be depressed *and* happy at the same time.

Smile

Did you know that it takes twice as many muscles to frown as it does to smile? I'm all for reducing wrinkles at the same time that I lower my stress. How about you? Try this: stand up, slouch with your head down, and frown. Let your arms hang as if you can't move them. How do you feel? Probably low-energy and down—that's because your body is in a negative position. Now stand up nice and tall. Wave your arms around and jump for joy while you smile. Immediately you will have more energy and feel better. By putting your body in a more positive position, you are setting yourself up to feel better. Throughout the day, check yourself. If you are slouching, sit up straight.

One evening driving home from work, I wondered why my rearview mirror was always out of position at night. Who was moving it? I then realized, as I looked at myself in the mirror, that I was sunk down in the seat and hunched over like an old man!

In the morning I sat up nice and tall. It wasn't the mirror that had moved; I wasn't in the same position at night because I slouched. Ironically, I would be exhausted when I arrived home. So I tried an experiment. I made a conscious effort to sit up straight on my car ride home at night, and you know what? I felt better—and I could use my mirror without moving it!

Wake up with a smile and go after life.... Live it, enjoy it, taste it, smell it, feel it.

—JOE KNAPP

Have Fun

What makes you smile? Sadly, the activities we enjoy the most are often the first things we stop doing when the stuff hits the fan or things get nuts. Try to weave back into your life something you love. Is it reading? Running? Knitting? Walking? Playing tennis? Visiting with friends? Whatever it is, make some time for it. Having fun will allow you to face the hard things in life with more enthusiasm. Visualize your energy as water in a cup. If you only pour it out, the cup will become empty rather quickly. You must do things to fill it back up. A little time spent on something you enjoy will give you extra energy to tackle difficult things.

Give a Little

In my own life, I realized how important it was for me to give to others when I was going through my divorce. I needed to focus on other people's problems, which made me realize how insignificant mine were by comparison.

Remember, God doesn't give us more than we can handle. You may be able to cope with something that would knock me to my knees, but I can deal with something that may be harder for you. All of us, though, benefit from giving back. A popular television commercial has a theme song, "Give a little love, and it all comes back to you." The ad features one man showing an act of kindness to a stranger. That stranger then does something for another stranger, and it gets passed along until the very end when the first man gets blessed. It came full circle.

"It is more blessed to give than to receive."
—ACTS 20:35 NIV

Be Love

I must really like the movie *Bruce Almighty*, because I'm going to quote it again. When God (Morgan Freeman) is talking to

Bruce (Jim Carey), he reminds Bruce that each of us should "be the miracle." We shouldn't sit there and wait on God to fix it for us; instead, we should try to fix it ourselves.

In the same way, we can "be love" to other people. We can be a light to the world and represent God. God works through you and me. If we are too stressed out to care for anyone else, then we are hindering God's plan. Do something for a neighbor. Bake them some cookies. Watch their dog. Call an elderly woman who is lonely and invite her to lunch. The world needs love; it needs you! And by giving, you will receive.

Know Your Limits

On the flip side of that is making sure you understand your own limits. For some of us, this is more difficult than for others. If you tend to give until it really hurts, you might benefit from the book *Growing Weary Doing Good?* by Karla Worley. Thinking only of others until you burn out isn't what God had in mind. Karla ended up in the hospital, and for months she couldn't be a wife, mother, sister, or friend. She learned that she had to set limits. The same is true for the rest of us. We have to know when enough is enough. What are the warning signs that you are totally spent? Do you get irritable? Are you short? Do you cry more frequently? Do you just want to sleep? Remember, you are just one person and can only do so much.

Protect Your Perimeter

A dear friend with whom I enjoy horseback riding made a CD of songs for me to use while trail riding. On it was the classic song "Don't Fence Me In," sung by Gene Autry. As appealing as the song is, it reminded me that sometimes fences can be useful.

Think of your emotional energy as open land. If you have no fences, your energy flows without any restrictions. That may be exhilarating, but it also means that your door is wide open to anyone at any time. Fences serve a purpose. They keep in what we treasure and keep out what might threaten us. We can open the gate for friends and loved ones, but we also will be able to protect ourselves.

Maintain Margins

Think of the margins on a sheet of paper. They frame our words. Without them, people wouldn't be able to comprehend what we wrote. White spaces on paper—and in our lives—are what give us breathing room. Don't fill up every page so full that you can't breathe.

Christmas is a perfect example. It is a wonderful time of year, but many of us fill our schedules so completely that we lose the spirit of the holiday. Don't let this happen for another Christmas!

This year, cut back on your Christmas activities and go for quality. Do name draws for the family instead of giving gifts to every person, and make the gift more meaningful. Create a Christmas web page that people can visit rather than mailing a newsletter. Print up address labels instead of writing them out.

Simplify not only Christmas but also everyday events. During the dinner hour with your family, let the calls go to voice mail. That is what it is for! Suggest to friends and acquaintances that they call ahead before visiting so you can have the opportunity to say yes or no. Remember, the more in charge of your life you are, the less stress you will have from being out of control.

Simplicity is an exact medium between too little and too much.
—Sir Joshua Reynolds

Set Boundaries

Have you ever said yes to something when you really wanted to say no? I think we all have. We need to say what we mean and mean what we say. Period.

*Say what you mean
and mean what you say*

A book that has dramatically changed my life is *Boundaries* by Henry Cloud and John Townsend. The premise is that we need to set boundaries in our relationships with family, friends, and coworkers. When do you say yes and when do you say no? It is different for each person, and every situation is different. We must be actively involved in the process in order to prevent getting stepped on or hurt.

When we say yes and we really wanted to say no, we aren't being authentic and true to ourselves. I know it's hard to say no, but we can soften the blow depending on how we say it. For example, if you are called by your child's teacher at eight o'clock in the evening and asked to bake twelve dozen cookies for the following day, you could say something like, "I could help out with a dozen or two." That doesn't sound like a no, but it is being realistic. If baking cookies is completely out of the question because of prior plans, then you might say something like this: "I would love to help next time if you could give me a little more notice." Wording can be the key to helping everyone feel OK.

Don't Forget to Say Yes

On the other end of the scale are some people who never say yes. In fact, we can all fall into this trap when stress is high. We say no to lunch with a friend, no to a massage that we desperately need, no to a nap—no to things that make us happy. Don't feel guilty about doing things for yourself. Remember Karla. She wasn't good for anyone when she burned out. So don't forget to say yes to the things that will energize you, renew you, and help you manage your stress.

Great things are not done by impulse, but by a series of small things brought together.

—Vincent van Gogh

Take Responsibility

Saying yes is really taking responsibility for ourselves instead of pointing the finger at others. If we are miserable, we really have no one to blame but ourselves. Don't get me wrong—I know people may have hurt you; I have been there. But we still have the choice as to how we will handle it. Being angry or withholding forgiveness hurts no one but us. It may feel good at the beginning, but it will eat you alive.

Acknowledge what you need and go after it. No one will think less of you or consider you selfish for caring for your own health. It is the responsible thing to do! Guess what happens when you are vibrant, healthy, strong, and positive? You have much more to give the world.

Shoot Straight

For those of you who are married, have you learned yet that your husband can't read your mind? No one can. It is up to us to tell our spouses what we need in very specific terms. How unfair is it to get upset at your mate for not doing something you need if they don't even know you need it? Don't expect your friends to come running to your aid if they don't even know you are hurt. Speak up, in love, about what is going on and what you need.

During an abusive marriage, I didn't tell a soul what I was going through. When I announced my divorce, friends were shocked; no, they were angry, because I hadn't told them what was happening. How could they be loving and supportive friends when they didn't know? Some of them read me the riot act, and I learned that I have to let some people in. With trusted family and friends, don't beat around the bush or drop hints; tell them straight up what is going on and what you need.

Be Authentic

Putting on an act doesn't help anyone. God made you who you are; don't be ashamed of it—flaunt it! Besides, trying to be someone else takes a lot of energy. The more you try to cover up things or be a different person, the more energy you are losing. I don't know about you, but I need every bit of energy I can get my hands on!

Be true to yourself. That may mean you need to reflect on who you really are, what matters to you, and what you stand for, and that is OK. It's easy to lose yourself along the way, especially if you have had children. You've been a wife, a mother, a sister, a friend (back to all the hats we can wear)...who are you for *you?*

Know Your Mission

What is your purpose? Why are you here? If you haven't asked these questions yet, you need to. God has put each of us on this planet for a reason. It isn't necessarily what you are doing at work or even at home; it is the contribution to the world that only you can make, no matter what your role or what you are doing. I encourage you to write a personal mission statement that includes who you are in Christ, what your purpose is, and why you are here. Keep it somewhere handy. I have mine in my planner, and I review it often to remind myself that God has plans for me. When we are aligned with God and our mission, we become energized.

When you discover your mission, you will feel its demand. It will fill you with enthusiasm and a burning desire to get to work on it.

—W. CLEMENT STONE

Be All You Can Be

You don't have to join the Army to be your best. I believe that living out every day to the fullest is our gift back to God. He gives us life—what are we doing with it? Don't hold back. If you want to be silly, be silly. If you want to try something new for the sake of trying something new, go for it! We don't get any do-overs in life. Make the most of it and experience all you can.

Breathe

All the while, don't forget to breathe. When things are hectic and busy, we begin to take short, shallow breaths. This doesn't give us enough oxygen, and it results in fatigue. It creates a vicious cycle and can lead to sickness. Take time to breathe deeply every day.

Here's a great way to practice breathing that will take your stress level down immediately (don't try this while you are driving):

- Sit up nice and tall, shoulders back and head forward.
- Take a deep breath from all the way down in your lungs; lift your arms up to your sides while you do it until they are over your head and you have counted to ten.
- Hold your breath and keep your arms over your head for five seconds.
- Slowly let your breath out as you lower your arms, counting to twenty.
- This gives you a chance to get all the bad, stale air out and the opportunity to fill your lungs back up with clean oxygen.
- Take regular breaths in and out.
- Repeat the process five times.

This exercise gives you a chance to get the stale air out and fill your lungs back up with fresh air. How did it make you feel? I can almost bet that you feel better and that your tension was reduced. If you try this in bed (you can omit the arms if you are lying down), you will probably fall asleep. This beats counting sheep every time!

Rest and Recharge

Resting is vital to stress management. Our brains work hard all day long. Sometimes the only time they actually get to rest is when we sleep. Even then, we can find it difficult to turn them off, can't we? Remember to breathe. Try a hot bath. A cup of chamomile tea works great for me right before bedtime. Whatever helps you calm down and rest, do it before you hit the hay.

Research shows that those who sleep at least seven hours a night are thinner than those who sleep less than seven hours. When you don't get enough sleep your body craves energy, and the way most people provide energy is through caffeine or sugar. The problem with these quick fixes is just that—they are fast to help but come crashing down just as fast. Good rest will provide your mind the strength it needs to function throughout the day without the junk.

We'll look at getting your health back in chapter 4, but for now, give your body some time to recharge. Our bodies, like our minds, can sometimes recover with a break. Stretching is an excellent way of helping the body after it has been taxed.

Renew

Don't forget your spirit through all of this. If your life has been out of control for a while, chances are that your spirit took a hit. Spend time with God, quiet, uninterrupted time just being with him. Develop a heart of gratitude for all you have, and pray for those who are less fortunate.

Listen

Don't forget to listen. How easy it is to do all the talking. Then we wonder why God hasn't answered us. Well, he was waiting for us to shut up! Listen to his small voice. God oftentimes isn't in noise and activity but in a whisper.

> *Then a great and powerful wind tore the mountains apart and shattered the rocks before the LORD, but the LORD was not in the wind. After the wind there was an earthquake, but the LORD was not in the earthquake. After the earthquake came a fire, but the LORD was not in the fire. And after the fire came a gentle whisper.*
>
> —1 KINGS 19:11-12 NIV

Reflect

In order for us really to listen, we must clear our minds. With all those hats we wear, this is more easily said than done. But meditation can help. Meditation is simply preparing yourself to receive from God and reflect on what he has for you. Use your breathing technique and sit somewhere warm and cozy. Be sure to allow yourself twenty to thirty minutes of uninterrupted time. Don't pray, don't talk, don't sing hymns in your head—just be.

I'll be honest with you; I find this extremely difficult! It takes practice, but we get points for trying. The more open and receptive we are, the less stress we will have inside of us, and the more of God. I find that instrumental music helps. Some meditate while doing yoga, but when I do yoga, I'm busy trying not to fall over! You do what works best for you.

Be a Good Friend

In the midst of your harried life, don't forget your friends. As I mentioned earlier, when our lives are out of control, we can say no to the wrong things. Be careful not to say no to friendship and *being* a friend. As a society, I think we are becoming too self-centered—that is, we have so much going on that we just don't have time for anyone but ourselves. We can have good intentions, but we never seem to do anything about them.

Make time for people. They are what matters. Pick up the phone to cheer up a discouraged friend; go to lunch to celebrate another friend's birthday; send a funny card just to say hello to a long-distance friend—do something. Stay connected within your circle. You will be blessed for it.

Circle of Influence

Lastly, I want to talk about your circle. Everyone has one. We have many things going on in our lives, and it's easy to worry and fret about them all. I want to suggest a better way to spend your energy.

Take a look at the circles below. The large circle represents your Circle of Concern. It includes *everything* you are concerned about: world peace, war, starvation in Africa, AIDS, killer bees, the drought, distant relatives. Everything. These are things you're concerned about but have little control over. Maybe your job is more powerful than mine. Maybe you even have top-secret clearance. But still, you can only do so much. The things in our Circle of Concern are in God's hands, and we are called to pray to him, not be him.

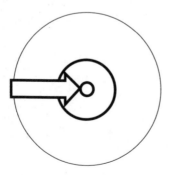

The second circle represents your Circle of Influence. These are things and people you can control or affect in some way, such as your family, neighborhood, community, and job. You can volunteer at the local shelter serving meals to homeless folks. You can vote and stay up-to-date on political issues. You can make sure your kids have all their shots. You can do something about your Circle of Influence, so why not spend more energy here? Spending energy worrying about what you cannot change is pointless. All you will get is tired, frustrated, stressed, and sick. Concentrate on what you *can* do.

Now let me ask you this: Can you make your family, friends, and coworkers do exactly what you want? No, but you can *influence* them. Because they respect, admire, and love you, they will consider it. But ultimately, the decision is theirs, isn't it? So do we really have control? Trying to control the world and the people in it will wear you out. Instead, try working on the only person you have complete control over: you.

The smallest circle is saved for us. It's called: My Attitude. Work on having a positive attitude no matter what, and you can be a change agent. Like smiles and laughter, positive attitudes are contagious.

Attitude is the speaker of our present; it is the prophet of our future.
—JOHN C. MAXWELL

Kick the Stress Habit

Anything new will take a little getting used to, but I encourage you to get out of your stressed-out rut. You can get used to things being the way they are, even when you aren't happy about it. You deserve so much better, and I want you to have your life back! Start with something easy and build from there. But start. OK?

Part Two

It's Time
for a Change!

3.

Of All the Things I've Lost, I Miss My Mind the Most!

I don't have Alzheimer's because I don't forget all the time. I must have 'someheimers' though. Sometimes I remember and sometimes I don't!

—AUTHOR

 Can you relate? The more stress you have, the more forgetful you will be. Ever go up the stairs to get something, but once you arrive you can't remember why you went up? Have you forgotten where you parked your car lately? Your body and brain can only take so much. If you are misplacing your keys on a regular basis or spacing out on doctor's or lunch appointments, then you need to slow down and do some mental work. Now, if you take off to the school and forget your children, well, you are beyond help! Only kidding. Stranger things have happened.

The movie *On Golden Pond* is adorable. If you haven't seen it, you'll enjoy the story about an aging couple struggling with the transitions of growing older together. In one scene, Norman, played by Henry Fonda, needs to make a phone call to town. Since he is at a lake house with limited telephone service, he needs to contact the operator. He does, and she puts him on hold, saying, "One moment, please, while I try to reach that party." Norman waits a few minutes. When his party is reached and says hello, Norman is taken back. "Who is this?" he curtly questions. The man on the other end of the line then asks, "Well, who is this?" After bantering back and forth a while, the man finally says to Norman, "Hey, you called me!" and hangs up. Poor Norman forgot that he made the call and why. It's a funny yet sobering scene. Stress will induce this type of forgetfulness *way* before your age would dictate it, so we really must get our lives back for our mental health, which in turn will help us create more balance.

A Balanced Life

We have talked about getting our life in balance, but we haven't really discussed what that means. Let me share with you how I look at it. Our vehicles have four tires. Those four tires provide a nice, comfortable, and safe ride when they are in good condition. Ever drive in the snow or rain with bald tires? Have you ever experienced a flat tire? It isn't a fun ride. I was on my way back from Los Angeles not too long ago, and a tire blew out. I was in the far-left lane going about seventy miles per hour, the speed limit. Traffic was heavy. I kept my cool, slowed down, and began maneuvering my way over to the shoulder. By the time I got to the side of the road, I was exhausted. Physically I had had to stay in control, and mentally I had had to keep it together. I was a wreck! Those few minutes felt like a lifetime. My ride was *not* smooth, and I was not a happy camper.

Our lives are a little bit like that car. We have four "tires": physical, mental, emotional, and spiritual health. As we are driving along in life, if we haven't serviced and cared for those four tires equally, we will not have a safe, enjoyable ride. And trust me, the ride will be draining.

Now, I know you feel like you can't possibly squeeze anything else into your life, but if you don't do some things differently, you will forever be behind the eight ball. In order to get out of the rut and increase your energy, you will have to break some old patterns. So I'm not really asking you to add things but rather to replace some old habits with better ones.

Many people give great attention to maybe two of the four tires but completely ignore the other two. I know I was out of balance during my divorce. I was exercising all the time and praying hard. But I was not taking care of my emotional and mental health. I was a mess—full of fear, hurt, guilt—you name it. If you recall the different types of stress, the hard times of life can really challenge us to stay in balance. But please try. I paid a price that I don't want you to pay. I want you healthy and strong! I know you have a ton going on in your life, but do not settle for addressing just one or two areas; go for total health and work on them all.

If you don't, your ride can become bumpy. Worse, you can have a total blowout. You may be shocked and surprised: "How could this happen?" Keep in mind that it is much easier *not* to be in balance than to be in balance. But anything of great value takes effort, and it will be worth it. I promise.

Anything of great value takes effort.

A client of mine had had enough of being miserable. After an ugly divorce, she felt betrayed and beaten down. As the years passed, she realized she hadn't let go of her anger. But she didn't know how. It was almost as if her anger kept her alive, and she was afraid that if she let it go her ex-husband would somehow win. When we met, she was negative and very unhappy. She was exercising and going to church, but she was not dealing with her mental and emotional baggage. So, she was given the assignment to write a letter to her ex and say the things that she never got to say. I encouraged her to be raw and honest, as no one would see this—not even me. Her next assignment was to go to the beach and burn the letter. I suggested that while the smoke floated into the air, she turn all those hurtful feelings over to God and let them go for good. After the letter was burned, she ran into the ocean to signify a new beginning. She never turned back. Once she felt harmony and balance in her life (all four tires in good condition), she committed to keeping it that way. Wait until you feel it!

> *"You will be secure, because there is hope."*
>
> —JOB 11:18

My goal in this book is to help you physically, mentally, emotionally, and spiritually. I want you to have a smooth ride, girlfriend! But, like our cars, we require regular maintenance. It will take looking at all areas of your life and doing a little bit every day. The good news is that a little bit will go a long way.

> *A little bit will go a long way.*

This chapter is designed to help you cope mentally. The suggestions and ideas are for you to consider as you move along the path of regaining your life. I want to keep things light and supportive. Take what works and apply it.

Get a Grip

Sometimes when things get bad, we must take a step back and evaluate what is going on. While we are in the thick of it, we can find it difficult to see the forest for the trees. Your first step, therefore, should be to S.T.O.P.

Stop
Think
Observe
Proceed

Whether you're in the middle of an argument with a spouse, a stressful debate at work, or trouble with your kids, *stop* long enough to assess the situation. Reacting without thinking can get us in trouble and create more stress, so *think* about what is happening. We have something between our ears called a brain; let's use it more often and think before we speak or act. We also have eyes, so *observe* how others are behaving and feeling. Any time we can put ourselves in their shoes, we will have more compassion and understanding. Then and only then, *proceed* and take your course of action.

Mistakes Happen

Alas, we are human, and occasionally we will stick our foot in our mouth or do the wrong thing. Instead of beating yourself up over it, learn from it. I think women are much harder on themselves than men, who seem to be able to file it away and move on. For many of my women friends, too much energy is wasted on the "shoulda, coulda, and wouldas" of life. Change gears and start putting energy into learning from your mistakes so you can do it better the next time.

How does God teach us to be patient? By giving us situations that try our patience! Trust me, God will present another opportunity for you. Practice makes perfect—or at least better.

Extend G.R.A.C.E.

Ever see the commercial that says, "We don't live near perfect. That's why there is Walgreen's"? Not one of us here on earth is perfect. The only perfect man was nailed to a tree. To expect others and ourselves to be perfect is unrealistic. Your children will make mistakes. Your friends will let you down. Your husband will hurt you by doing or saying the wrong thing. Don't put pressure on those you love to be perfect. Instead, give them some grace and understanding.

We must allow people to be who they are and to do the best

they can, which is all any of us can do. It doesn't mean you should let people deliberately injure you or slack off from responsibilities, but it does mean you should weigh what is truly important.

Ladies, I think that sometimes we are awful about expecting the things be done our way, especially in the house. If your husband vacuums but doesn't do as good a job as you would, concentrate on his gift and not on how he did. If your son or daughter puts the dishes away but in the wrong place, thank them, don't scold them. Extend G.R.A.C.E.

Give
Respect.
Appreciate and
Compliment
Efforts

Give People the Benefit of the Doubt

Be sure to think the best of people. Do not focus on the fact that they will make a mistake, but expect the best of them. Marriage therapists will tell you that if you want your husband to be a better man, expect him to be. When we know for a fact that he will forget to pick up milk on the way home from work, he *will* forget. If we can guarantee that he will be grumpy on date night, he will be grumpy.

I believe one of our greatest responsibilities to our husbands is to give them the benefit of the doubt. I'm speaking from experience, because I haven't always given that to my husband. Coming from an abusive ex-husband, I think deep down inside I expected that my new husband would eventually wound me too. This was a recipe for disaster! I expected him to be a jerk, and he was at times. I finally had to own up to my part and begin thinking positively about him. Once I expected better from him, he gave it to me.

As a man thinketh in his heart, so is he.

—James Allen

Think Positively

Thinking positively has power. I play tennis, and for the longest time I would yell at myself in my head when I made mistakes. I would call myself names like "stupid" or "idiot" every time my shot didn't go where I wanted it to. My game would go from bad to worse, and I would get so frustrated that I didn't want to play anymore. Then I read *The Inner Game of Tennis* by W. Timothy Gallwey. His book doesn't tell you *how* to play tennis but *what* to think. He has similar books on just about every sport. What he teaches is to not attack yourself when you make a mistake but instead to address the mistake.

For instance, when I hit the ball too low, I need to correct my swing to make the ball clear the net. Or if I hit the ball too long and it goes out of the court, I need to adjust my power a bit to keep it in. Focus on what you need to do differently rather than tearing yourself apart. The world will make plenty of attempts to drag you down; you don't need to join in.

If you find yourself repeating the same mistake over and over again, look at it objectively. What are you doing wrong? What could you do differently? Getting on your own case won't help you overcome the mistake. In fact, it will probably ensure that you remain stuck. But thinking positively can help you move on.

Repeat After Me

Years ago, a friend taught me three powerful words: up until now. Perhaps you have been losing your temper with your children...up until now. Maybe you have been slacking off on exercising...up until now. Or your life might be out of balance...up until now! By using these three simple words, you can set your brain up for a change. Your brain hears the past tense and is already looking toward the future.

Change is the law of life, and those who look only to the past or the present are certain to miss the future.
—JOHN F. KENNEDY

Look Forward, Not Back

Speaking of the future, don't look back. Yes, we need to know our past mistakes so that we can learn from them, but don't get stuck there. We all make mistakes. Name them, acknowledge them, and move on. Too often, we spend our energies worrying about what we may not be able to become, instead of becoming it.

Ever find yourself saying, "I do not want to become my mother"? Or "I don't want a marriage like my in-laws' "? Don't concentrate on what you lack or don't want to become; instead, focus your energies on developing yourself and adding those things to your life that you want. By focusing on the negative, we are only looking at what isn't working or what we don't like. We have to put on new glasses and begin looking for the things we do like and want.

Know What You Want

But we must first know what we want—what we really want. What matters to you the most? What kind of life do you want? When you embarked on getting your life back, what did you have in mind? I'm not talking about general statements like peace, love, and joy. Of course we want those, but what do they look like in real life? The more specific we get, the clearer the picture in our minds of what we are aiming for.

I knew that I didn't want my second marriage to be like my first one, but I didn't have a clear picture of what a good marriage looked like. Then God put a wonderful Christian couple in my life who became my example. I started to look at what made their marriage work and used those traits as my benchmark. We'll never hit the target if we don't know what it looks like, so let's take a moment and have you check the words that signify what you want rather than looking at where you are right now. Check all that apply (they are in no special order):

- Healthy conflict
- Civil disagreements
- Respect of differing opinions
- Acceptance of who I am today
- Encouragement to grow
- Honest prayer
- Heartfelt gratitude
- Appreciation
- Support
- Thoughtfulness
- Kindness
- Partnership
- Shared responsibility of household chores
- Engaged conversations
- Intimacy
- Closeness
- Other

The list could go on and on, but at least this is a start. Visualize the kind of life and marriage you want and keep these in the forefront of your mind. Toss out the negative images and replace them with your future life!

You Are God's Child

Other images we need to get rid of are pictures of ourselves that do not reflect the way God sees us. I don't know about you, but I have struggled with my appearance all of my life. I don't see what God sees; I see all my flaws and flab. God has created us, and he doesn't make junk. But the media will try to tell us we aren't good enough. They plaster images of rail-thin models in advertisements and sell products that promise to make us look like them. Combine these images with the very mixed-up world where looks are more important than good health, and it is no wonder we aren't sure of ourselves.

Well, ladies, it's time to get a new mirror! Don't use the one you bought at the store, but instead use God's reflection. He loves you just as you are today, wrinkles and all! Accept it as truth. If you have a hard time believing it, keep thanking God for creating you. Accepting God's love can take the pressure off *how* we look and put the emphasis on *who* created us. When we do that, we can appreciate that we have been put on this earth for a reason, and that trumps our outward appearance.

Of course, God does want us to be healthy, and we'll talk about that in the next chapter. But we aren't what we look like. We aren't even what we do.

 ## You Matter

Men in particular seem to struggle with their identity outside of what they do. Their job or career *is* who they are, and when they retire they often don't know what to do. Statistically, a high percentage of men die within their first year of retirement. I fear that women are getting caught up in this same identity issue. We are wives, mothers, sisters, friends, executives, volunteers...an array of hats, remember? We give to others in all sorts of ways, and we can get suckered into believing that who we are is defined by what we do. But it is not. Who we are is much bigger than that. God wants us, not our accomplishments.

In 1997, when I almost couldn't move because my weight had dropped to ninety-seven pounds, I almost lost hope. But God provided me a vision. I've never had that happen before or since; it was like watching a movie but without sound, and I was in it!

I saw myself walking down a dirt road. I was extremely tired from the divorce; I was hungry; I was overwhelmed with grief over my mom's death, and I was lugging all my belongings in one massive black suitcase on wheels. I could barely move it, and I was crying uncontrollably. I would take a few steps and then would drop the suitcase because it was just too heavy. I sobbed harder and fell to the ground. As I wailed in anguish, I exclaimed, "I can't go on! I can't do this anymore." My head fell into my hands.

Moments later, I saw two dusty feet in canvas sandals through my hands. As I looked at them, I could tell they had walked a lot of miles. I lifted my head slowly and saw a worn-out robe tied with a rope. Suddenly, I found myself looking into the eyes of Jesus. His eyes soothed me immediately. Without a word, he pulled me up off the ground and wrapped his arms around me. As he held me closer, my weeping grew deeper—straight from my soul.

All the things I had done and not done rushed through me. A list of things I was supposed to do hit me like bricks. Jesus began walking me down the road, but I stopped. I forgot my bag, which was still on the ground behind us. I turned to reach for my stuff, but he shook his head no. He drew me close, right to his heart. And from his heart I heard this, "You are what matters to me, not your material possessions or what you do." The message poured from his heart into mine, and we began walking again. I left the suitcase behind, and my tears subsided. I began to regain strength. At eight o'clock that night, I got out of bed (I had been physically unable to before) and began a life of handling my stress better. I've never been the same since.

God loves *you*. Knowing that you don't have to perform for him should dramatically reduce your stress. We put pressure on ourselves, but instead we need to love ourselves as he loves us.

Love is the highest, purest, most precious of all spiritual things. It will draw out from men their magnificent potential.

—ZIG ZIGLAR

Love Thyself

I think loving ourselves is more easily said than done, though. But thankfully, God is a great example! No matter what, he loves us. Why is it that we can extend such unconditional love to our husbands, children, and friends but find it difficult to be good to ourselves? Well, that needs to change. And besides, if we want to continue to love others, we have to start by loving ourselves so we have love to give away. Love starts with accepting yourself. You are good. If you have trouble swallowing that, then repeat after me: *You are good enough for today!* We are all growing and improving, but you are good enough for today.

You are good enough for today.

Inside of you, you have what it takes to get through whatever you are facing. God won't let you walk through it alone. You are strong and courageous...you are woman! What are some ways that you can show yourself love? Here are some quick suggestions, but you know what works for you:

- Pick up some flowers for yourself
- Eat a cookie or two
- Sip on your favorite hot tea
- Get a pedicure
- Take a nap
- Make a candlelight dinner for you

- Listen to soothing music
- Relax
- Read a good book
- Look through old photo albums and reminisce
- Create a scrapbook of your recent accomplishments
- Hang out in a hammock
- Go shopping
- Work on a craft you enjoy
- Get a massage
- Go for a run or bike ride
- Hit the spa
- Have a long lunch with a friend
- Fill in the blank _____

If you haven't done one of these in a long while, you are overdue. I recently had a massage, and boy, did I need it. Don't put yourself last on the list all the time. In order for you to continue wearing all your hats, you have to keep yourself healthy.

Be Mindful

The decision to change has to be yours. I am certainly here to coach, guide, and encourage you, but you have to want to do this. If the pain is great, then chances are that you are ready to make a change for the better. But if things are just so-so, you may not be as inclined to do something about it. Well, don't wait for things to explode! Take charge now! Besides having a clear picture of what you want your future to look like, know why you are doing this.

Your motivation is the key to success. In order to get where you want to go, you must stay committed. Think about the people in your life—your children, husband, family, friends. How does your life affect them when you are stressed and overwhelmed and when you are calm and balanced?

You heard my testimony about how stress nearly killed me. I'm highly motivated now to manage it the best I can every day. I want to be healthy in all areas. I wish that for you as well. If you want to see your kids graduate college and live their lives, you must make changes today. If you want to walk the beaches with your husband during your golden years, then you'd better be making steps toward a more balanced life now. If you desire to be all God wants you to be and fulfill your purpose, then you are called to manage your life the best you can.

Remember, none of us is perfect. But we can make steps toward being a healthy person mentally, emotionally, physically, and spiritually. Believe in yourself, and you are on your way!

4.

Whose Body Is This I'm Living In?

Without discipline, there's no life at all.

—KATHARINE HEPBURN

 Did you see the remake of the movie *Freaky Friday*? Lindsay Lohan plays Jamie Lee Curtis's daughter. They aren't getting along, and they fight at a Chinese restaurant one night. With a little Hollywood magic (and your imagination), their fortune cookies switch their spirits. Lindsay's character moves into her mother's body, and vice versa. Jamie Lee Curtis, being the mom, is actually excited to have a youthful body again. The scene where she is checking out her own buttocks in the mirror is hilarious! Poor Lindsay Lohan screams at the sight—well, what she can see with her horrible vision—of her wrinkles and flab. It's a shock, and she can't believe her mom lives in this body. How does her mom even function?

Well, ladies, you might be wondering who switched your spirit and how you ended up in "this body"! Was it the body snatchers? Sorry, no. Welcome to middle age. If you aren't there yet, it will come. Even if you are younger, you might not have the body you want right now. In either case, it is a bit freaky waking up one morning and seeing a body that surely belongs to someone else!

I know of a lady who looks great for her age, which is in her sixties. Well, the time had come for her to finally get glasses. She had been fighting it for some time. She picked out a very cute pair, and when the new glasses with her prescription arrived, she shouted, "Holy cow! When did those wrinkles show up?" The blessing of her poor vision had been that she couldn't see the wrinkles creeping in as a natural part of the aging process. Suddenly she could see—really see! She was quite surprised to look at herself with her new eyes.

I love the story of the lady who is walking along the street and senses someone following her. She turns her head, and sure enough, something is there. She walks a little faster and turns her head again. It's still there! The faster she walks, the more it moves. She suddenly realizes it isn't a person but her big behind swaying from side to side! Ha! How easily this can happen. As we age, things aren't quite where they used to be. Our bottoms can be down by our knees and our, eh-hem, boobs can be at our waist. But have hope! We can create a different shape by toning up and trimming down. What you see today doesn't have to be your future.

What You See *Isn't* What You Get

I remember my mom complaining about her gray hairs. They made her feel old. I thought they looked cool—like highlights. Today, we have such great options for coloring that you can literally "wash that gray right out of your hair," as the commercial claims. But some things take a little more time to fix. Oh, the weight-loss industry would like you to buy into their quick fixes, but believe me, they don't exist. If any one of those quick fixes actually worked, we wouldn't need another weight-loss product ever again! Instead of giving them your money, which is all they really want, spend your energy and time on getting healthy the right way.

The good news is that you can change your body. You aren't stuck with where you are today, and it won't take as long as you think to change it. It won't happen overnight, but it *will* happen. Have faith.

> *"If you have faith as small as a mustard seed, you can say to this mountain, 'Move from here to there' and it will move. Nothing will be impossible for you."*
> —MATTHEW 17:20-21

I enjoy Joel Osteen's television program. He is known for saying that we should concentrate not on how big our problems are but rather on how big our God is! Amen to that! Although being overweight, out of shape, or in poor health can feel humongous right now, small steps will make a huge difference. That is what this chapter is about: small things that can make a significant difference in your overall health. This isn't a health book. If you need coaching on that, please pick up one of my books, *Finally Fit* or *Fit Over 50*. They give specifics on cardiovascular exercise, weight training, and proper nutrition. They have tons of pictures to show you correct and safe form, ensuring that you will get the most out of your efforts.

This book, by contrast, has been on the lighter side and will now focus on your physical health, one of the four "tires" of your overall well-being. I will definitely provide you with good information on exercise and nutrition, but I will also encourage and uplift you. Most people know what they need to do, but they have trouble doing it. Others may be confused about what is really the best approach. We'll address a little bit of a lot of things, in hopes of getting you to spend some time on your physical health along with your emotional, mental, and spiritual health.

Remember, it is all about balance. I teach fitness classes to those who are fifty and older. I have seen the members of my class get healthy. First their blood pressure goes down and then their cholesterol. Finally, the weight comes off. Some of these people had never exercised a day in their life until they were over sixty years old. They were able to do it, and so can you! God is on your side, and so am I.

 ## Start Inside Out

Good health does start from the inside out. A sixty-year-old woman in my class was frustrated that she hadn't lost a pound and had been exercising religiously for months. I asked her how she felt, and she replied, "I haven't felt this good in twenty years!" My comment back to her was, "Well, then, you are already healthier on the inside. The weight *will* come off. Trust me." About a month later, she gave me a big hug. She had lost ten pounds. She has since lost thirty pounds and looks fabulous! Her doctors are amazed at her blood pressure and cholesterol numbers, which are like those of a thirty-year-old.

Your energy will increase well before you lose a single pound. Internal health should be our goal to begin with. Of course, if we happen to shed a few pounds in the process and fit in smaller jeans, that's terrific! But remember, we don't all have to look the same and be a size two. How grateful I am for that! God loves us just the way we are, but we do need to get physically healthy.

Our lives are a sum total of the choices we have made.
—Dr. Wayne Dyer

If it's not motivation enough to be healthy for yourself, think of the loved ones in your life. Remember that they need you. In order to be a wife, mother, sister, friend, good neighbor, or ambassador for Christ, you need your health.

Fit vs. Healthy

What exactly does good health look like? Skinny jeans have made a comeback, I'm sorry to say. Frankly, I never have fit into those ridiculous things, even when I was a teenager! Being thin isn't always healthy. While some women are blessed with tight, narrow legs, others who fit into skinny jeans are just too thin. They have lost weight, but they also have lost critical muscle. This, in turn, is setting them up for osteoporosis and other diseases down the road. I am shocked to see how many young people are so thin that they would blow away with the slightest wind. We need muscles to survive and be strong. If you have daughters, please encourage them toward health, not the latest style. Our teenage years are critical to our golden years, meaning that what we do or don't do when we are young will have an impact on our health later in life. Thin does not equal healthy in every case. Now, those who are thin but also lift weights, thus creating muscle tone, are healthy . . . but I bet they don't fit into skinny jeans! The skin-and-bones look is not healthy, no matter what the magazines say.

On the flip side, every person who has a few extra pounds isn't necessarily unhealthy. Some people just carry more weight than others. And some don't want to go the extra mile to achieve super tone; they are content with healthy insides and a little flab on the outside. One of my clients has a potbelly, but he is in excellent condition. In order for him to get rid of that spare tire, he would have to commit more days to exercise and change his eating habits further. He is happy where he is, and he is very healthy.

Our problem is that we worship and idolize thin people. Everywhere we go, we are bombarded with images of what I call "twiggy" girls—you know the type . . . they look like Olive Oyl in the old Popeye comic strip. In addition, we have a tendency to compare ourselves with other women. I wish we could be more like men in this regard. They seem to be able to look at other men and appreciate features without tearing themselves down. My husband can see another man's six-pack abs and go, "Wow, he works out and looks good." He will leave it at that. He won't go into a massive depression because he doesn't look like that. It is what it is. Period. But we women tend to see only our flaws and other women's best features. Ugh!

We consider thin to be healthy, but I as mentioned, that is not always the case. In fact, fit people can be unhealthy too. I've been to countless fitness workshops where a stick-figured young woman gets her body fat tested, and it is in the red zone—meaning that more than 40 percent of her body is fat! How could a size two have that much fat, you ask? If she isn't eating right and isn't exercising, she is unhealthy. She may be a size two because she is twenty years old. Wait until she is thirty! I guarantee you, those who are banking on being thin when they are older simply because they were thin when they were younger are in for a surprise. The remedy is simple, because the formula is the same for us all: we must eat right and exercise. Then and only then will we be healthy.

Healthy looks different on each of us. We won't weigh the same or carry our weight the same, but we all must have low blood pressure, good cholesterol numbers, and normal body fat.

Target Your Healthy Weight

I'm not a big fan of scales, because muscle weighs more than fat. Did you know that? Do you know why? As you build muscle, the fibers are splitting apart and growing, becoming more compact. Fat cells are fluffy and full. They take up more space but weigh less. Compare a marshmallow to a jellybean. Jellybeans are harder and more compact. One jellybean weighs more than one marshmallow, but the marshmallow takes up a lot more space. Does that give you a visual? Anyway, scales are evil! Too many women get sucked into weighing every day and freaking out when they gain a pound. I was one of those women, and it stressed me out. Want to reduce your stress today? Throw out your scale! Your weight will fluctuate throughout the day. Focus on doing the right things and fitting into a certain size clothing you want instead of reaching a number on the scale. But, if you must weigh in, do it at the same time every day. Even then, however, your weight may vary depending on factors such as hydration. In any case, realize that it is just a number.

All that said, a scale does give us a starting point. It also helps us determine body fat. If you haven't been measured in a while (or never), I encourage you to visit your health care professional for a reading. Understanding your body fat percentages, along with other specific data regarding your unique health issues, will help you develop a safe plan—one that will move you toward better health.

Waist-to-Hip Ratio

Additional information that will help you and your health care professional is the Waist-to-Hip Ratio. *ScienceDaily* (August 15, 2007, "Waist-to-Hip Ratio May Better Predict Cardiovascular Risk than Body Mass Index," accessed via www.sciencedaily.com on April 1, 2008) shared a study by *The Journal of the American College of Cardiology* that found people with a larger waist-to-hip ratio may be at an increased risk of heart disease. Everyone is different, but consider this yet another piece of the puzzle. Your physician should be able to pull all the pieces together and give you a clear picture of your current health status. Measure your waist and hip, and provide the numbers in the blanks below. Take this to your doctor, and always get his or her approval before you begin any new exercise program.

Waist measurement (WM) = _____

Hip measurement (HM) = _____

WM _____ divided by HM _____ = _____ Ratio

If the ratio is greater than .95 for men, you are at *higher* risk. I'd encourage you to lose weight under the guidance of your physician or fitness professional.

If the ratio is greater than .85 for women, you are at *higher* risk. I'd encourage you to lose weight under the guidance of your physician or fitness professional.

Your Solution

OK, so you may need to lose some weight. You may need to lose a lot of weight. Let's turn our attention toward what you can do to change that rather than focus on how you got there. As I said before, the good news is that it won't take you nearly as long to improve your health as it did to destroy it. Don't beat yourself up. That would just be a waste of valuable energy. And don't let Satan attack you. If you have struggled with your weight for most of your life, read Psalm 46. God is your refuge and strength. You are not alone, my friend.

Here's what you need to do: burn more calories than you take in. That is it. No magical or secret pill exists—just a basic truth that applies to all of us.

Burn more calories than you take in.

Unfortunately, most Americans are taking in over 3,000 calories a day. Most women require from 1,300 to 1,800 calories. That difference is turning to fat, and once fat is stored, the cells remain forever. That doesn't mean they can't shrink, but we are stuck with those buggers for life. One of our goals, then, is to prevent the formation of fat cells in the first place. Keep your calories within your range. If you take in more calories than you want, work hard at shrinking the number and avoid adding to the problem.

To find out how many calories you need, take your desired weight and multiply it by thirteen. To achieve that weight, deduct 400 calories from your total. This gives you a target number of calories to take in per day—your daily caloric intake. Break that number down into the number of meals you eat each day, and you will have a caloric intake target for each meal (Peg Jordan, ed., *Fitness Theory & Practice* [Sherman Oaks, Calif.: Aerobics and Fitness Association of America, 1997], p. 244).

Read Labels

Not all calories are created equal. Just because something says "low fat," doesn't mean it is good for you. As you are shopping, keep in mind that product packaging is designed to make you buy the product; the manufacturer doesn't necessarily have your best interest in mind. Read labels. When something is low in fat, manufacturers have typically added more sugar, and vice versa. When products have a bunch of words you cannot pronounce, walk away. Try to eat things that are more natural. Food is fuel for your body. You wouldn't put junk in your gas tank and expect your car to run smoothly, would you? Be smart about what you put in your body, and your body will be happier.

Quick List for a More Healthful Lifestyle

You do want to consume more nutritious calories versus empty ones. Junk food has that name for a reason. It doesn't have any nutritional value, yet we get massive calories from it. All those calories do is add to our waistline! Here's a quick list to get you started on a more healthful lifestyle.

- Do not smoke
- Drink alcohol in moderation
- Avoid all fried foods
- Skip white breads and opt for wheat and grain breads
- Pass up sugary drinks and select low-calorie options
- Limit packaged foods and eat more whole foods
- Choose fresh over frozen when you can and frozen over canned
- Select lean cuts of meat
- Stay clear of sugar as much as possible
- Make homemade meals as often as you can
- Try to limit your portions to the size of your palm

- Drink plenty of water
- Eat your salad first
- Go light on condiments such as salad dressing and ketchup
- Say no to dessert
- Get plenty of rest
- Keep a positive attitude
- Pray

Learn to use ten minutes intelligently. It will pay you huge dividends.

—WILLIAM A. IRWIN

Fit It In

One of the questions I am often asked is "When should I exercise?" Some research has shown that exercising first thing in the morning will help set your metabolism for the day, and if you exercise before you eat breakfast, you will burn extra fat. However, additional research shows that exercising at the end of the day will help you burn off stress, which we already know can make us sick. My answer: exercise whenever you can squeeze it in. Exercising at any time is better than not exercising at all.

Do What You Can

Ladies, don't get hung up on doing this perfectly. If you do, you will probably sit around a very long time. Life is life. It will always throw us curveballs. Have you ever noticed that when you finally commit to doing something for yourself that you know you need, a crisis pops up? A kid gets sick. Your job goes haywire. I've seen it happen countless times with clients. They just begin an exercise program, and they sprain an ankle or have a car accident. I don't have any proof, but personally I believe Satan is to blame. Think of it... when we are sick and tired, we aren't a threat. But when we are one hundred percent gang-busters, fired up for Christ, we are a power to reckon with! Of course, Satan doesn't want us healthy. Be prepared for resistance, and don't put too much pressure on yourself.

Start Slowly

At the beginning of your exercise program, don't go crazy with it. Simple things such as walking are a great start. Build up to jogging and then running. If all you can do is ten minutes to start, good for you! Just do it. A former client of mine was an all-or-nothing person. Can you relate? For years she would be so disciplined with her nutrition and exercise that her entire life revolved around it. But then she would fall hard, completely disregarding all exercise and proper nutrition principles. She would yo-yo from ideal weight to forty pounds overweight. This isn't good for you, and it confuses your body. I would much rather see you do something in moderation, so you can continue it for the long term.

Go the Distance

Being healthy isn't an event. We have to get out of our heads that we are just shaping up for a wedding or high school reunion. We are doing this for life; you are doing this for *your* life. Good health isn't something we do and then stop. It is an everyday occurrence. The more you do it, the easier it gets.

Did you see the movie *Sleepless in Seattle*, with Tom Hanks and Meg Ryan? When Tom's character is on the phone with a radio host after his wife died, he shares how difficult it has been moving on after the loss. In this very touching scene, he says that his plan is to "get up out of bed every day and remember to breathe in and out." Then in time, he hopes, one day he won't have to remind himself to breathe in and out.

A healthy lifestyle is going to take effort. You will have to remind yourself every day what a good thing it is and why you are doing it. Over time, it will become a habit. I promise. You just have to stick with it.

 # Make It a Habit

I can be your friend and companion
or immediately turn into your enemy if me you abandon.
I can push you onward and help you set sail
or I can hold you back only to fail.
Friend or foe...only you know.

If you turn things over to me,
I'll get them done quickly, you'll see.
I'm easy to manage, but you'll need to be firm.
Just show me precisely what you want, and I will learn.

I have run with giants...each and every one.
But huge failures, I have also done.
I can make you great,
but know what is at stake.
I can be your foe or your friend.
You ultimately decide in the end.

Use me for whatever you want, I care not.
Just remember whom I am...forget not!
I am a habit, bringing the world to your feet,
or unraveling everything into massive defeat.

Treat me wisely and with great care.
Ignore me only if you dare. —Author

As you create new habits, I encourage you to not just pull things from your diet but to replace them with more healthy options. For those who have quit smoking or drinking alcohol, you know it is difficult to go cold turkey. A more effective approach is to replace a bad habit with a positive one. Here are some suggestions:

Instead of this	Do this
Coffee with all the "stuff"	Regular coffee. Better yet, drink hot tea!
Greasy hamburger and French fries	Veggie burger with a side salad
Bagel with cream cheese for breakfast	English muffin with low-sugar jam
Bag of fattening chips	Low-salt pretzels
Popcorn with butter	Popcorn without the butter (you'll save hundreds of calories!)

I think you get the picture here. Don't just give up something. You will probably miss it, crave it, and ultimately eat it. Replace it with something better and make a habit of it.

Do the Best You Can

Eat healthy foods as often as possible. By making smart choices most of the time, you will be free to live a little. I don't subscribe to a diet that focuses only on restrictions. If I tell you not to think of the color blue, what happens? You see blue in everything! Our brains immediately go to the places where we tell them not to go. Don't set yourself up for failure and discouragement. Instead, give yourself some wiggle room. Allow yourself four meals a week that can be less than ideal. Maybe it's eating a modest slice of cake on a friend's birthday, or toasting someone's anniversary with champagne. The amazing thing is that when you do have some freedom, you won't completely fall off the wagon.

Today Is a New Day

If you do goof up, start again tomorrow. One of the biggest mistakes people make is giving up after making wrong choices. So what; that was yesterday! Today is a brand new day that God has given us. He has already forgotten our wrongdoings, so let's move on! Our goal, of course, is to try and not have too many bad days.

Plan B

A great way to prevent bad days is to have some alternatives. If you plan to hit the gym after work but end up staying late at the office, what is your backup? Will you jump rope? Will you go for a run? Will you swim? Will you watch an exercise DVD at home? If you have in mind what you will do just in case, your chances of skipping a day will decrease significantly.

Stretch Yourself

Never, ever forget to stretch. We should all be stretching every day. Cats are a super example of stretching. They do it every time they get up to move. I know your life may not allow for that, but at least stretch after exercising. Besides helping your muscles return to a relaxed state, which will help prevent injuries, stretching is good for your mind, emotions, and spirit.

Speaking of stretching, some of this chapter might be brand new to you. Much of it probably isn't, but you may not have been applying it. Head knowledge isn't action. I do hope, however, that we have been able to help get you motivated, encouraged, and inspired so you will take some steps—any steps—toward improving your physical health.

Don't Delay

Although it is never too late to get healthy, don't delay starting on the path to wellness until you have a massive heart attack or are diagnosed with diabetes or a terminal illness. Start today; start now! This is your life. Make it a healthy one!

5.

Take a Number!

The easiest kind of relationship for me is with ten thousand people. The hardest is with one.

—Joan Baez

 Relationships: you and I have a lot of them. Hollywood has made several movies about families who merge together and end up with a dozen or so children. Movies such as *Cheaper by the Dozen* with Steve Martin, or *Yours, Mine and Ours*, remade in 2005 with Dennis Quaid, are often hilarious because of the mischief the children get into and the overwhelming feeling the parents have in trying to keep track of everyone. Those movies stress me out, because I can't even imagine that many intimate relationships! A husband, two cats, siblings, friends, and clients are plenty for me. I don't know how large your family is, but I do know that no matter how big or small it is, you have relationship demands placed upon you. And those relationships can cause stress. Remember the commercial "Calgon, take me away"? Some days, we wish we could be taken away from everyone to some exotic location.

All those hats we discussed in the introduction involve relationships. And relationships take work. Ever see the movie *Multiplicity* with Michael Keaton? He can't keep up with work and home demands, so he copies himself. He loves having a second self so much that he reproduces himself again and again. He's able to be everywhere and with everyone at the same time. Now admit it; you are thinking that this would be the best gift ever! You could truly bring home the bacon *and* fry it up in a pan, all the while never letting your husband forget he's a man! Well, Michael Keaton's character thought it would be perfect too. The problem is that each of his duplicates handles things differently and doesn't communicate with the others. Instead of his relationships improving, they get worse. More of us isn't the answer and won't solve our woes. When it comes to relationships, what counts is *quality*.

Right now, you probably feel that the relationships you do have take too much time; how could you possibly give more? Yet at the same time, you may feel isolated. It is not uncommon for us to feel we are being tugged on by a million people, without feeling connected to any single one. When we let quantity get out of control in this way, we become spread too thin, and quality suffers.

The goal of this chapter is to help you with your relationships, which are not all created equal. Some energize you, while others drain you. This chapter will help you evaluate who you are spending time with and how much time you are spending, then give you strategies for building stronger, healthier relationships. God designed us for connection; we need each other. But, we need to be healthy.

Seek Healthy Relationships

When we have healthy relationships, we have joy and energy. Think back to a time when you had a wonderful visit with a dear friend. You most likely felt renewed and reenergized after your time together. Compare that with a time when you had a conflict with your neighbor or a meeting with a coworker with whom you were at odds. After these kinds of interactions, you probably felt drained. We are given only so much energy every day.

Some of us are blessed with more than others, but however much we have, it has its limits. If we give it all away and save none for ourselves, we end up stressed and sick—it's called burned out!

Let's look at your relationships for a minute. How do you get along with your spouse or mate? How about with your children, parents, siblings, extended family, and in-laws? Then we have our friends, coworkers, church members, and on and on. Somewhere in that list is a person you are not getting along with, and it is sucking the life right out of you.

My mother told me when I was young that my siblings were family by blood, but it didn't mean we would automatically be best friends. She wisely advised me not to put that kind of pressure on the relationship. If I did, I'd probably be disappointed. Television shows like *The Waltons* portray "the perfect family," but it rarely exists. We can spend a lifetime trying to make our family fit the television mold, but we will just end up frustrated and worn out. What we need to learn is to manage our expectations and put our energy into the right relationships.

If you expect perfection from other people, your whole life is a series of disappointments, grumbling and complaints. If, on the contrary, you pitch your expectations low, taking folks as the inefficient creatures which they are, you are frequently surprised by having them perform better than you had hoped.

—BRUCE BARTON

Know Thyself

Managing our expectations requires us to look inward first. For those who are single and would like to be married, let me say this: it's better to be single than married to the wrong person! Being single can at times be lonely, but being miserable is painful and stressful. I have known too many women who married because they desperately wanted children, so they settled. Everyone lost, especially the children.

In order to avoid marrying Mr. Wrong, you must first know yourself. What are you looking for in a mate? For those who have already walked down the aisle, having a clear picture of what matters to you can help your new relationship. In some cases, you may realize why you have tension. For example, if you married a non-Christian and Christianity was high on your priority list, you can't expect him to change. You can hope and pray, but you married him as he was, and accepting this will reduce your conflict. Instead, look at the areas where you match up well and build on those.

We can learn a lot from online dating services. They understand the premise of matching up one's values with those of another person to increase our chances of success. What are the top ten qualities you're looking for in a relationship as a single? What are the top ten you're seeking in a mate when you get married? What values do you hold in esteem with your family and friends? Make a list. Some qualities on your list might be: Christian, athletic, smart, outgoing, faithful, honest, funny, trustworthy.

My Top Ten List

_____   _____
_____   _____
_____   _____
_____   _____
_____   _____

Look in the Mirror

I heard someone say once that disappointment is expectations not met. That hit me between the eyes. Too often, we blame others for our disappointments when the reality is that we didn't get what *we* wanted. Ouch. This made me reflect on arguments I've had with my husband. How many times was I mad simply because I didn't get it my way? "My Way" may be fine for Frank Sinatra, but in the real world we must compromise. If we value the relationship, we must sometimes put it first over our own needs.

Managing expectations involves taking a look in the mirror. After all, we are the common denominator in all our relationships. No matter where we run, we keep showing up! Ever try to run away when things weren't going well, hoping that a new location might make things better? Guess what—no matter where we run, we bring our own issues, desires, and demands with us, and we're just as likely to impose them on others.

> *At the heart of personality is the need to feel a sense of being lovable, without having to qualify for that acceptance.*
> —MAURICE WAGNER

Start evaluating your relationships to determine if you have been expecting too much. People can only be who they are and do what they know. Turtles don't fly! If you try to make a turtle soar like an eagle, the turtle will finally retreat into its shell in disgust, and all you will get is irritated.

As we evaluate our relationships, we should also check to see if we have been expecting our men to be more like us. God didn't want us to be exactly the same. We are supposed to be like a hand and glove, fitting together. Try accepting the "turtle" as he is, and learn to appreciate him for what he brings to the relationship. When we give unconditional love like this, often people will try harder to improve. They will feel more loved, and you won't have near the stress. Everyone wins!

Turtles can't fly.

Take Inventory

Besides expecting people to be what we want them to be, we can also put our energy into the wrong people. This is a tough one, because some of us want to love all and be good to all. This is an admirable goal, but even Jesus couldn't minister to his own village! We have to admit our limitations. Men have their egos when it comes to career, sports, and macho stuff. I believe many women have their egos when it comes to relationships; we believe we can do it all. Well, if you are overweight, stressed, tired, or sick, your body is telling you that you can't do it all. Accept it. This doesn't mean you are a failure; you are simply human.

I've been working on this very thing, and you know what? It is actually a relief to stop pressuring myself to be perfect. Oh, in my head I knew very well that I would never be perfect, but literally to stop *trying* gave me a wonderful sense of freedom.

So, who are you giving too much of yourself to? I want you to take some inventory here. We've looked at ways to see our possessions in their proper perspective; now let's do the same for our relationships. Under each heading below, list your relationships, how much time you spend on them (high or low), and whether they are energizing or draining (yes or no):

Immediate Family Members	Time Spent	Energizes Me	Drains Me

Extended Family Members	Time Spent	Energizes Me	Drains Me

Friends   Time Spent   Energizes Me   Drains Me

_____   _____   _____   _____
_____   _____   _____   _____
_____   _____   _____   _____
_____   _____   _____   _____
_____   _____   _____   _____

Coworkers   Time Spent   Energizes Me   Drains Me

_____   _____   _____   _____
_____   _____   _____   _____
_____   _____   _____   _____
_____   _____   _____   _____
_____   _____   _____   _____

Church Members   Time Spent   Energizes Me   Drains Me

_____   _____   _____   _____
_____   _____   _____   _____
_____   _____   _____   _____
_____   _____   _____   _____
_____   _____   _____   _____

Others   Time Spent   Energizes Me   Drains Me

_____   _____   _____   _____
_____   _____   _____   _____
_____   _____   _____   _____
_____   _____   _____   _____
_____   _____   _____   _____

Choose Wisely

When my husband and I first moved to Southern California, we didn't know anyone. A couple was kind enough to befriend us and help us with our move. We were grateful for their invitations to dinner, but every time we saw them, we fought. One night, we talked about it and realized that the other couple was toxic. They were negative people, complaining about everything and each other. They argued in front of us, called each other names, and showed no respect or love toward one another. They were sucking out our positive life force! When we evaluated this relationship, we realized we were spending too much time with the wrong people. We withdrew and eventually never saw the couple again. We had to move on and find healthy couples to associate with. Do you have anyone like that on your list? Here's the tough question: is anyone in your family like that? You can't disown your family, but you can set boundaries and margins, as described in the chapter 2. (You might want to review those principles again if you need to reinforce them.) Just because the person is a family member doesn't mean you have to subject yourself to extreme stress.

Do you struggle with your in-laws or your spouse's siblings? It is common to have some strain with a family you didn't grow up with. They may operate differently from the way your family does. We get in trouble when we expect our spouse's family to adapt to our ways, assuming arrogantly that our way is better than theirs. We can also get in trouble when they expect us to change without question and to adopt their family rituals. Neither case is healthy. We need to respect their family's traditions, and vice versa. When it comes to in-laws, you won't ever change them, so stop trying! Learn to live with them the best you can, and set some boundaries for yourself. For example, if the subject of politics is too emotional and stressful because of extreme differences, make a rule to never discuss it. Period. Most people respect boundaries when you set them. They want to honor your boundaries and support you. If they don't, then you've learned something about them and may want to spend even less time with them.

I believe that God has great plans for you. Why would you want to jeopardize those plans by losing valuable energy? Just as we need to avoid inappropriate behaviors and things of this world, we should watch the kinds of relationships we have and attempt to build healthy ones. A good way to do this is to spend more time around positive influences. Is there someone you adore who is loving and kind but who you aren't spending much time with? If she energizes you, make the time! The people on your list who give you energy are priceless. They help fill up your cup so you can go out to the world and give. They support and encourage you while you serve out your mission. Unfortunately, when we are out of balance, healthy relationships seem to be the first thing we relinquish. Maybe it is because we know we can, that those people will stand behind us even if we aren't investing in them at the moment. Perhaps we don't want to burden them with our troubles and stresses, or we might think we don't deserve them. In any case, I'll say it again: make the time! People and relationships are what matter. We need to choose our friends wisely.

> *God has given us two incredible things: absolutely awesome ability and freedom of choice. The tragedy is that, for the most part, many of us have refused them both.*
>
> —FRANK DONNELLY

Invest Wisely

A big movement in the business world right now is "getting the right people in the right seats on the right bus." I believe this expression applies to our personal lives as well. Life is a journey. Who do you want to travel with? Do you want negative people who bring you down or positive ones who lift you up? Life is too short to be with the wrong people. At work, you may feel you have to tolerate them, but in your personal life, you absolutely have a choice.

Ever been on a long flight and had a complainer sitting next to you? Everything is going bad for them, and everyone is mistreating them. They aren't happy about their seat, where they are going, or what they are doing. This makes for a very long flight! It can be the same in life. I'm not advocating being mean and dumping people in your life if they make a mistake. We all make mistakes, and that is what grace is for. But if someone is constantly dragging you down, consider spending time with someone else.

Once you find the right people, you must start investing in them. Relationships should go both ways. Want a true friend? Be one!

Want a true friend? Be one!

We can't expect people to give all the time, any more than we can write a check when our bank account is zero. We must invest in the lives of our friends. Certainly none of us gives because we want to take—that is not our motive. But we should be making "deposits." What have you done lately for that special person who means so much to you? How have you shown a friend that you care? From the lists you made above, please make another list, putting the name of at least one person from each category who energizes you. Rate how well you're doing in developing each relationship (0 to 10, with 10 being excellent) and add what you plan to do to improve it.

Name	Category	Quality	Plan

_____ _____ _____ _____
_____ _____ _____ _____
_____ _____ _____ _____
_____ _____ _____ _____
_____ _____ _____ _____

Love that lasts involves a real and genuine concern for others as persons, for their values as they feel them, for their development and growth.

—EVELYN DUVALL

Build a Foundation

Have you read the book *The Five Love Languages* by Gary Chapman? If you haven't, I encourage you to read it. He outlines ways in which each of us prefers to be loved and supported. Just as we all have unique personalities, we also have different needs. Some of us prefer gifts, while others need quality time. Others seek verbal affirmation. Understanding the people in your life and what matters to them will help you build a solid foundation and invest in your friends in a manner that works for them. We certainly get points for trying, but when we nail it, we get huge points!

I love it when my husband does things for me without asking—washing my car, fixing the lights in the garage, mowing the grass, dumping the garbage. These things make me happy. In contrast, what makes my husband happy is verbal compliments. He's thrilled when I use words to express my appreciation to him. Well, during our first years of marriage, I was doing things for him without saying anything, and he was using words to compliment my every move. We both felt unappreciated! Finally we realized that we both were trying to make each other happy, but we were doing it in ways that worked for *us*. If you can discover what makes your husband, children, family, and friends happy, then you can give them gifts they will appreciate. Your relationships will be stronger and healthier.

Be Generous

I see a tragic pattern in society. People are living as if they don't have enough time, energy, or love to go around, so they retreat. They can't be bothered with others. I see it with parents of young children, who seem to feel that they can't possibly do anything but raise their kids. Hmmm...then how did our mothers do it? I see it in women who have big, high-paying corporate jobs. Some of them feel that work is so important that they can't do anything else. Sadly, our society is creating more of these people every day.

When we think only of ourselves and don't reach out to others, the world becomes a cold and unfriendly place. Those around us begin to feel the scarcity and may retreat further. It's a vicious cycle. I encourage you to be generous with your smiles and laughs. These are free but can make you and others feel so much better. Be giving with compliments and courtesies such as "please" and "thank you." These don't take much effort but can immediately establish a positive rapport. Be patient and kind. Be available. Yes, all of us are busy, but we need to be available for the situations God presents to us. If we are effectively managing our time, emotions, thoughts, and relationships, we will be able to reach out more effectively to help and serve.

> *When one door closes, another opens. But we often look so long and so regretfully upon the closed door that we do not see the one which has been opened for us.*
>
> —HELEN KELLER

Create a Healthy Home

When thinking of others, don't forget your family. Home is a place to feel loved and safe. It is our refuge, and women have traditionally had a special role in making it so. Because I know how difficult this role can be, I have offered ways to help you reduce your stress, become more balanced, and feel happier.

We may laugh at the saying, but it's true: When mama ain't happy, ain't no one happy! We have that kind of influence over our families, and we need to take it seriously. We need to monitor ourselves. So let me ask you a few questions:

- Are you on edge?
- Are you overly critical?
- Are you annoyed, angry, or upset most of the time?

If so, then you picked up this book at the right time! You may feel as if you are on the brink of burnout; I'm here to help.

Start journaling. You may have journaled in the past, but I want you to change the way you do it. I want this to be a "joy journal." I want you to start concentrating on what is wonderful about your husband and family, not what is driving you crazy. By journaling in this way, you can begin to change your attitude and create a more positive environment for everyone.

And don't forget your pets! Pets truly love us unconditionally. They don't care what we look like or what we own. Not only do they love us; they help our families. Children who are raised with animals are much more well-adjusted, confident, and healthy.

Keep the Flame Going

What turns your husband on? What rocks his boat? Save enough of yourself to give to him. Life will always present challenges. We have to maintain, nurture, and develop our relationships *despite* what is going on. I think we can be guilty of putting our husbands on hold "until things settle down." All of a sudden, the years have gone by, and we look at our husbands and say, "Now, who are you?" Don't let this happen. I've seen it in other marriages, and it is tough to rebound—not impossible, but tough.

What kinds of things make your husband smile? Jot down a list of them here and then commit to doing one per week for a month.

My Honey-Do List

_____   _____

_____   _____

_____   _____

_____   _____

_____   _____

The amount of satisfaction you get from life depends largely on your own ingenuity, self-sufficiency, and resourcefulness. People who wait around for life to supply their satisfactions usually find boredom instead.

—DR. WILLIAM MENNINGER

Live Life to the Fullest

Relationships are ever changing. A dear friend says that they are like an onion. When you peel one layer off, you have another layer. We will constantly be learning and growing, and that means we are alive. Celebrate your victories and learn from your mistakes because that is really all any of us can do. The good news, I hope, is that you have more tools now to help improve your relationships. As you apply them, your quality of life will go up, and your stress will go down. I'm rooting for you!

We're not going to stop there, so follow me to the next chapter as we look at other aspects of your life.

Part Three

It's Time
to Take Charge!

6.

I Am Woman, Hear Me Snore!

This—this was what made life: a moment of quiet, the water falling in the fountain, a girl's voice . . . a moment of captured beauty. He who is truly wise will never permit such moments to escape.

—LOUIS L'AMOUR

 What was your favorite thing to do as a little girl? Did you like playing with your dolls? Did you enjoy making mud pies? Did you dress up or give musical performances? I loved watching clouds. I would lie on the grass and see the different shapes: elephants, kitty cats, butterflies, and even dragons, with the wind continually changing the formations into something else. I would get lost in those clouds for hours. As we get older, we outgrow many of our favorite activities, but we never get too old to enjoy simple pleasures. Yet life never seems to allow the time for such frivolous activities. We are climbing corporate ladders, running car pools, volunteering on boards, attending PTA meetings, cooking dinner, and making our houses homes. Whew! We are beat. Forget soaring to great heights; we are happy to snore at home in bed!

When we consider all the hats we wear, sometimes life can be overwhelming. And of course, all of us are intimidated by the wife "worth far more than rubies" who is described in Proverbs 31. Slowly, though, perhaps we can begin looking realistically at ourselves and deciding how we can take small steps toward taking charge of our lives. It isn't easy, but it *is* doable.

Maybe one place to look is at our animals. Here's a list of the top ten things we can learn from our pets:

1. Be excited about the ride
2. Never pass up an opportunity to lie in the sun and get fresh air
3. Jump for joy when loved ones come home
4. Behave and do what you are told
5. Speak up when someone has stepped across the line
6. Nap often
7. Run, jump, and play every day
8. Eat well so you can live well
9. Be faithful to those you love
10. Just be yourself

No matter what your age, a little girl lives inside you who longs for the simple life, to play, love, and enjoy. To truly balance our lives, we must first acknowledge her and then love her. Loving her means giving in to some simple pleasures such as family, friends, and fun. It also means getting ourselves right spiritually.

This chapter will explore how to tap into your childhood dreams without sacrificing your duties. God loves the little children, and really, we are all his children. When we are in God's presence, we are little girls looking up to our Heavenly Father in awe and admiration. We must keep a piece of that little girl alive in order for our relationship with him to be pure, wholesome, and respectful. Otherwise, we are asleep at the wheel.

Let us savour the swift delights of the most beautiful of our days!
—ALPHONSE DE LAMARTINE

Reconnect with Your Maker

Remember our discussion about life being like a car with four tires? Spirituality represents the fourth tire. We are never complete without our relationship to God. If you are depressed, stressed, or sick, take a look at that relationship. Are you close to God or have you pulled away? He doesn't leave us; we are the ones who retreat. He loves us no matter what we do or don't do, so if you have fears, concerns, or issues, take them to God.

I know some folks have been hurt by the church and are apprehensive about God. Church is not God. God-fearing people *attend* church, but God's spirit lives inside each of us. Don't blame God for a bad experience you have had with people. People can do us harm because they make mistakes. Consider this: if you are stressed out and upset, other people probably are as well. Walking wounded—that is us—all of us! If we look solely to one another for help, we will be discouraged and defeated. But if we turn to God, he will not forsake us, let us down, or hurt us. He will be our rock and refuge! He promises that. Start reconnecting with God, even if only in small steps. Start off by saying how grateful you are for your life.

A grateful heart is a happy heart!

Be Grateful

Even if your life has had challenges, it is *your* life, and God gave it to you. What an awesome gift. Thank him for it. Do you have a roof over your head? Do you have food to eat? Clothes to wear? Be thankful because some people do not have even these basics. Extend appreciation for the people in your life and their health. Too often, we take our blessings for granted. In fact, make a list of everyone you are thankful for right now:

I Am Thankful For...

_____   _____
_____   _____
_____   _____
_____   _____
_____   _____
_____   _____
_____   _____

My father died when I was thirteen years old. My mother was a single parent before it was common or was even called that. She wore the same clothes for most of my childhood life. She couldn't give me much, but she gave what she had and could afford. She never complained but considered herself blessed to have her children.

To realize the value of a friend, lose one.

—Unknown

In times of difficulty, always ask, "What is good about this?" God doesn't point his almighty finger at us to make us pay, but he does promise that good things *will* come out of our adversity. I've just spent the last three years in treatment for Lyme Disease, which is on top of the six years of bizarre symptoms and pain during which the illness was undiagnosed. I've had some dark days, but God's strength has pulled me through. And he has given me some amazing gifts as a result: compassion, understanding, support, love, and the ability to extend grace to myself. I've always been one to raise the bar high for myself. Sure, I can encourage others to be easy on themselves, but I had to really practice that on myself this last year. I learned it was OK to rest and ask for help. What has God given *you* this past year? Take a minute to write down a few of your challenges and the blessings that resulted from them.

Challenge	Blessings
_____	_____
_____	_____
_____	_____
_____	_____

If you are in the midst of a tough time, you may not be able to see the blessing yet, and that is totally OK. Trust God that the blessing will come, even though you don't know what it looks like just yet.

Let Go and Let God

Thank God again for all he has given you. When we focus on the good and turn over the bad to God, we have more energy to move ahead. I don't know about you, but my load gets awfully heavy sometimes. Let God carry it. Taking on too much between work and home? Let go of some things. Refer back to the Circle of Influence that you filled in earlier and remind yourself that you can really only change yourself. Focus on that concept and your relationship with God, and you will see greater results: inner peace, improved health, and renewed energy.

With that thought in mind, consider some of the things you are worrying about. In the table below, list some of the things (work and home) that are keeping you awake at night. Then reflect on whether you can change them. If you can, list the action required (talk to someone, get help). If you can't, write in the words: *Let God!*

Issue	Can I change?	Action required	Let God!
_____	_____	_____	_____
_____	_____	_____	_____
_____	_____	_____	_____
_____	_____	_____	_____

Trust God

Over lunch recently, I was talking with some friends about how it can be easier to turn things over to God but harder to let him keep them. How true! We somehow think we understand things more thoroughly and can handle them better than God. Or we panic and think God may not have time for it. We are so wrong. Just as we delegate assignments at work, we must not only turn over our struggles to God but also turn over the authority to do something about them. (Of course, God has the authority, but if we want to withhold it, he lets us.) Have you ever been in a position where you were given a task without the authority to get it done? It is frustrating and counterproductive. We want less stress and more balance, right? Well, when we give something to God, let him keep it. Save your energy for something else.

 # Be a Light

Whether we work at an office or at home, all of us have influence. In order to create a healthier world, we must, as Mahatma Gandhi said, "be the change we want to see." Unhappy at home? Create the type of home you want and pour out your love to all! Want a better work environment? Stop complaining about what isn't happening and become a part of the solution. We are all leaders, no matter what our role. In fact, someone this very minute is probably looking up to you for something! (See my book with Dr. John Jackson entitled *Leveraging Your Leadership Style.*)

Start a trend of kindness and thoughtfulness. Here is a list of rules to live by, whether at work or at home:

- Say something kind to several people every day
- Smile and say hello to everyone you see

- If you want good friends, be one
- Don't be a dream- or hope-stealer—that may be all some-
one has to hold onto
- Pray with honor and respect
- Be a tender warrior
- Give, and then give some more
- Be a promise keeper, not a promise breaker

Decide, Discipline, and Do

Keeping promises is vital to healthy relationships, both at
work and home. Before you say yes to something, remember the
three Ds: *Decide, Discipline,* and *Do.* First, you *decide* in a deliberate way. To do this, you weigh the pros and cons, using the
Opportunity Scale, until you are sure you want or need to do
this over everything else being considered. At that point, your
decision becomes a promise. Skip this step at your own peril.
When we don't think matters through to make sound decisions,
we can end up feeling stressed, overwhelmed, and even bitter.
Next, in order to fulfill the promise you have made, you must
discipline yourself by taking the correct measures and steps to
honor your word. Do you need to research something, talk to
someone, get help, or acquire the tools to make it happen?
Gather what you need, then *do* it!

Words are not action. So often, people say they will do something and then don't follow through. People will be counting on
you. When you let them down, trust is broken, and trust takes
time to rebuild.

Words are not action.

Ever ask your husband to pick up the dry cleaning, and he
forgets? It is a small thing, but it can wear on you over time.
Why am I bringing this up? Because when we have broken trust
and strained relationships, we have stress. Want to get further

ahead at work? Be trustworthy. Want a deeper relationship with friends and more intimacy at home? Be honest. And always, always, honor your commitments. Do not be afraid to narrow down your obligations. More isn't always better. In fact, as I get older, I've come to realize that in many cases, less is more! Choose quality over quantity and see your stress come down.

Balance Your Budget

This is one message our society certainly isn't preaching. Everyone seems to be pushing their finances to the red line. Commercials encourage us to buy everything we want *now* and to do everything today. What happened to planning and looking forward to the future? I recently saw an ad in a local bank that read, "You deserve everything you want now, so get a home equity loan and get all your toys!" Folks, debt causes stress! I believe that finances are still the number-one cause of divorce in this country. Be smart. We must learn to enjoy the process of saving and delaying gratification.

Make Your House a Home

As women, we often are the ones who create home. We establish traditions, provide a warm environment, and care for our loved ones. Do not take this role lightly. Think back to your childhood and your fondest memories. Chances are that your mom was instrumental in making them. If you have a job, do not let home suffer. I know this takes effort, but family *is* more important than any job. Believe me, I love to work. I consider it an honor to use my God-given gifts, but I also know I am called to love my husband.

God made women different from men. Many of us are softer, gentler, and more sensitive to things that cannot be seen but only felt by the heart. These are good things! Yes, we can perform just as well as men in most things, but we have our own unique gifts and talents. Don't be ashamed of them or hide them—flaunt them!

Here are some strategies for keeping the stress down at home:

- Live within your means: create a budget and honor it
- Watch your mouth: be kind and avoid harsh or critical words
- Be a better listener than a talker
- Say you are sorry and mean it
- Do not hold things in but express them in love
- Manage your task well so you can enjoy the people
- Never put off until tomorrow what you can do today—get it done!
- Protect mealtime and other family times
- Show respect
- Do not nag
- Forgive and move on
- Say please and thank you
- Stop blaming others and take responsibility for what you have or have not done
- Give hugs away any chance you can get
- Take at least one family vacation a year
- Create holiday traditions
- Show your patriotism
- Say "I love you" often

Dream and Desire

I think we all have a vision of what the perfect family would be. We have been dreaming of it since we were little girls, along with the perfect wedding and the perfect house. All those romance movies and novels can certainly put unrealistic thoughts in our heads. It's great to dream, but we must distinguish between dreams and desires. When we start comparing our family with others or what we see on television, we are crossing a line. In doing so, we can become disgruntled and miserable to live with, and that isn't good for anyone.

Many dreams are simply fantasies. You may dream of becoming a supermodel, but if you are over the age of thirty without any experience, your chances are not good. On the other hand, wanting to be fit, trim, and healthy is not just a dream but a desire—and an attainable one! I'm not trying to discourage you from dreaming, because I believe we can do amazing things with God's help; *but* we should discern what we want and what is possible.

> *Since it doesn't cost a dime to dream, you'll never shortchange yourself when you stretch your imagination.*
> —ROBERT SCHULLER

Be There

Dreams keep us alive . . . dreaming of something better for others, for the world, and for ourselves. Of course we need to escape sometimes, but when we return, be in the moment that is real.

Have you ever zoned out at a meeting and missed something important? Have you ignored what your child was telling you because you spaced out for a second? Daydreaming can be healthy, but when you can, be actively involved. Pay attention and listen intentionally. Mirror back what someone said so you can ensure you heard them correctly. Ask questions to keep yourself engaged.

Work

When at work, be fully engaged. One of the most difficult things for anyone to do—perhaps especially for women—is to stop multitasking and focus. We juggle a million things at once. We sometimes have trouble leaving our personal life at home. But if we want more balance, we need to be more effective while on the job. Make the most of those hours at work—get it done and get out of there!

> *The ability to concentrate and to use your time well is everything.*
> —LEE IACOCCA

Are you working a lot of overtime? I know that in some cases the load is just too great and the people too few. In other cases, the long hours are a way of hiding from an unhappy home life. In still others, if we are honest with ourselves, it's because we're not organized, and so it takes longer to complete the tasks at hand. No one is going to take care of you and your life; you must stand up for yourself! That means doing your job and doing it well.

When at work, give a hundred percent so that you can leave and enjoy what really matters, your personal life. Leave work at the office. Let it stay there, where it belongs. If you find yourself talking or thinking about work all the time, evaluate your job. Should you switch positions, leave the company, or try a different career? Work is supposed to support our life, not *be* our life. I've had personal experience with this one. I loved what I was doing, but that didn't mean I should do so much of it that I sacrificed other things—like my health. It is indeed a juggling act—with fireballs! But let me say this: work will *always* be there, but your health can leave you.

> *Work will always be there, but your health can leave you.*

Work is part of life. Most of us must work. But we need to balance it very carefully with our personal life. Here are some tips for climbing the corporate ladder without getting stepped on or sacrificing your health or family:

115

- Communicate well and often
- Be professional and courteous at all times
- Lead by example
- Establish boundaries and protect them
- Stay focused and alert
- Create a plan and work the plan
- Be prompt
- Respect others
- Devise systems to serve you, not the other way around
- Do what works but be willing to change if a better way comes along
- Be a team player but know your individual strengths
- Don't be afraid to toot your own horn
- Document, document, and document
- Keep a clean desk
- Prepare so that you can be confident
- Celebrate your victories

When you know what you want and you want it badly enough, you will find the ways to get it.

—JIM ROHN

Be All You Can Be

Probably all of us have met some version of the Proverbs 31 woman, the wife "worth far more than rubies." She basically runs her own business, provides income for the family, meets her husband's needs, cares for her loved ones, and treats everyone fairly. She is a cornerstone in the community to boot! Instead of being intimidated by her, let's try to learn from her. I do not believe God told us about her to discourage us but rather to show us an example of what is truly possible when we put our life in balance.

The reality, ladies, is that we are already doing these things anyway. We may not feel in control of them or feel that we are doing a very good job, but we are doing them. As you take steps to reduce stress and create more harmony in your life, you will begin to see aspects of the Proverbs 31 woman develop more fully in you. Just wait, and you will experience the transition from feeling as if you never have enough time to feeling that you can take on the world—not tomorrow or the next day, perhaps, but in time. As we all learn, grow, mature, and age, we become more of what God wants us to be rather than what we thought we should be. The process of discerning what we really want—and what God wants—can dramatically change our lives.

You are well on your way to creating a healthier life for yourself. The final chapter will share encouragement, inspiration, and stories to keep you on the path.

7.

That's Life

Life is not a destination; it's a journey. It's not a series of goals; it's a series of steps, of events unfolding as you make your way. Life is not all about accomplishment; it's about doing, participating, progressing, growing, and learning.

—MIKE HERNACKI

 I'm a tennis player. I picked the game up right out of high school and have been playing ever since. It's a great game because you can play the rest of your life. In my twenties I played singles aggressively and often. In my forties I still play singles but more strategically. Friends I know in their sixties play doubles for sheer fun and exercise. Life has stages, doesn't it? We are constantly moving from one stage to another. We start off as a baby, then become a toddler, then go on to the tween and teenage years. Young adulthood turns us toward being wives, mothers, and bosses, among many other hats. Just when we have one stage figured out, we are on to the next one: empty nester, grandmother, and retired.

No matter what your stage is, life is like a tennis match. We can learn so much from the game, even if we don't play it. In this chapter I want to share some of the things tennis has taught me about life, along with other inspirational stories to encourage you on your journey.

I am thankful that God doesn't expect us to be perfect...right now! It is a process. We are forever evolving into something better. God extends grace to us as we fumble our way through and he loves us, but he is constantly guiding us and directing us toward improvement. He is the perfect coach!

Listen to Your Coach

Coaches can make or break a team. The movie *Glory Road* is about an average team that gets a coach who wants to take the team to their full potential. He pushes them hard but emphasizes a team concept. In the end, they become champions and win! We all have a champion inside of us. And we have the world's best coach. Like any athlete, we must listen to our coach's advice. He gets paid the big bucks for a reason. Well, God is God, and he knows his stuff! Listening requires us to shut up long enough to hear God. I don't know about you, but I can get so busy praying that I don't listen for the answer. The first step is to listen.

After listening, we must go and do it. You've probably heard the story before, but it's good so I'll tell it again. During a horrendous flood, a man refused to evacuate his home. The police came to escort him out, and he said, "That's OK. God will save me." The police left, and the water level kept rising. Pretty soon a rescue worker in a boat came by to offer a ride. The man again replied, "That's OK. God will save me." By this time the water was so high that the man was sitting on his roof. A helicopter team hovered over him, yelling, "Grab hold of the rope and we'll pull you in." He screamed back, "That's OK. God will save me." Well, the man drowned. When he reached heaven and saw God, he was a bit miffed. "God, I believed in you. Why didn't you save me?" God calmly answered, "Son, I sent you the police and a boat and a helicopter. What more did you want?"

Although God is all-powerful, he has given us abilities and expects us to use them. It is not enough to pray and listen; we must act on what God reveals to us. Thankfully, he doesn't expect us to go it alone.

Friends in your life are like pillars on your porch. Sometimes they hold you up, and sometimes they lean on you. Sometimes it's just enough to know they're standing by.

—Anonymous

Pick Your Partners Wisely

Playing tennis requires at least one other person to play with, and in doubles you need a partner. Oh, sure, you can hit a ball against a wall all by yourself, but it isn't the same or as much fun! We weren't designed to walk this journey of life alone. In tennis, your opponent can strengthen your game. In life, true friends sharpen your iron, and vice versa.

Do you have a solid friendship with someone you trust and feel comfortable with? In our attempts to do it all, we can forgo deep, meaningful relationships and replace them with superficial or surface ones. They are easy but not rewarding. Make the time to play with the right people. When you play with a person who seems mean or dishonest, you will not enjoy the game. When you can, pick partners who have *your* best interests at heart.

Equip Yourself Properly

As a tennis player, I have learned that having the right equipment for my level of play really does make a difference. If I have the right size and weight racquet along with proper shoes, my strokes have a greater likelihood of being solid. Life is no different. We need the right equipment to get through. What kind of life you want depends on the tools you will need, but I suggest that a Bible is the foundation. The answers to your questions lie in those pages. It's the ultimate authority on personal development!

What else do you need? Parenting tips? Marriage help? Strategies on how to care for your aging parents? We are all in different places and stages. Maybe you need a college degree or second language for your career. Perhaps some conflict-resolution classes would assist you in dealing with your teenager. If you are struggling with an addiction, seek help. Regardless of the type of life you lead, use the RTP model (resources, time, and people) to help you identify what you need in life. Then make it a point to get what you need. But remember, all the tools in the world won't make a difference if you don't use them.

A woman I know had all the tools: good education, solid job, family, friends, house, and health. Then she started drinking, and it got out of hand. Before she knew it, she was a full-blown alcoholic and had lost everything. She had to discover new tools in order to piece her life together. She rebelled against God for a while, but when she almost died from alcohol poisoning, she realized how far off the right path she had gone. She didn't want that life anymore; she wanted better. She turned to God, and he began to give her strength. But she had to use those tools faithfully and do the work. Today, she is in a better place than she ever was before! We all have the ability to live at our full potential.

 ## Play at All Levels

How *is* your game? Are you playing at the highest level possible or settling for average? We can all get comfortable in life. Before we know it, we can become mediocre. Yikes! God knew we would struggle and had some things to say about it:

> *I know your deeds, that you are neither cold nor hot. I wish you were either one or the other! So, because you are lukewarm—neither hot nor cold—I am about to spit you out of my mouth.*
> —REVELATION 3:15

Judging from this scripture, it's pretty clear that we need to be fired up, living life to the fullest and giving it our all! In tennis, the way to do that is to play against opponents at all levels: people of greater skill, of equal skill, and of lesser skill. This same approach can be helpful in life.

First, we need people in our lives who are where we want to be, living the kind of balanced life we strive for. Do you know someone to look up to? For me, a pastor and his wife from my childhood have been instrumental in my life. They have been incredible examples of faith, love, and integrity. If you don't have someone like this, ask God to provide you with a person who can mentor you. Your parents may be your mentors, and that is great. But if you are like me and no longer have your parents, others can fill that role. If you had a bad example in your life, find people you admire and study them to learn what it takes to have a quality life. Work on those traits. In tennis, when you play a stronger player, you get better. In life it takes more work and effort, but the payoff is huge—emotional, mental, physical, and spiritual growth.

Second, we should have peers with whom we can share life, enjoy the game, and maintain our level of play. It isn't humanly possible to play full-throttle all the time. Even the pros need breaks. The people in this second group are your kindred spirits. I must confess, though, that these people can be the hardest to find. If you have them, treasure them. Shows such as *Friends* and *Seinfeld* make it look so easy to have a group of peers who are your equals. Don't be discouraged if you are still developing these relationships. They take time. My favorite memories of tennis are not the games in which I slaughtered someone on the court, but the ones where the games were so close that we never knew who would win. We were evenly matched...in our zone. Remember, God gives us life. We should enjoy it!

Finally, it isn't all about us—well, it shouldn't be. We should also have younger people in our lives. In some cases, we may actually be younger in age but more mature in our faith or level of play. We all have a duty to give back what we have been given, sharing our wisdom and experience. And besides, when we play with those who aren't quite as good as we are, we get a little boost. In tennis, it is totally a confidence builder to win easily. In life, we can reflect on where we once were and be pleased to see our progress. How far we have come!

> *The lesson that most of us on this voyage never learn but can never quite forget is that to win is sometimes to lose.*
> —JOHN WOODEN

Winning Isn't Everything

Now, I do like to win. You probably gathered that about me already. However, winning shouldn't be the main focus. When I was younger, it was. In fact, I recall a tennis game with a peer that was so intense that we kept playing even though it started to rain. Neither of us wanted to admit we should stop, as it would show weakness. So we kept playing. The raindrops got larger and began coming down in sheets. Before we knew it, we were sliding on the court. The ball was skipping and leaking water! We kept belting it, because winning was the objective. I have since matured and have learned that although winning is great fun, it isn't everything. I mean, if anything is worth doing, it is worth doing well—but not at the expense of others.

Trying too hard to win in other areas of life can also cause problems. Be careful. Whether it is winning awards at work, building frequent flyer miles, obtaining merit badges for your kids, or having the cleanest house on the block, be sure to keep your perspective. These things are not bad in and of themselves, but when we obsess over them, they can wreak havoc on those we love and ourselves. Pause a minute and evaluate yourself. Where in your life have you put winning as the objective?

I have to constantly work on this. I'm a recovering perfectionist. Unfortunately, I haven't found a twelve-step program for Type A personalities, because we'd show up and want to conquer the twelve steps on the first night! Seriously, I have discovered an approach that has helped me with this issue, and that's to focus on the difference between perfectionism and excellence. When we try to be perfect, we are in essence saying, "Hey, look at how great I am!" We are doing things to get marks on the board, stars on our papers, and accolades from friends. Perfectionism is the end goal. When we strive for excellence, however, we are honoring God. We are doing the very best we can with what we have and then letting go, turning the results over to him. Our desire is to be our best, but the outcome is his. The attention is not on what *we* did but on God's plan.

Leave the Temper Tantrums to John McEnroe

I don't know about you, but I need my sleep. I can handle pressing deadlines and urgent requests, but if I don't get my sleep, my ability diminishes greatly. I get stressed and short-tempered. What sets you off? If you are already stressed about something, your ability to cope with something else will be reduced. Don't let it get the best of you; instead, practice some of the stress tips outlined in this book. Do whatever works for you, as long as it is healthy. When we lose control, we lose more than our temper.

I adore the movie *When Harry Met Sally* with Meg Ryan and Billy Crystal. It is a great story of two friends who over the years become lovers. In one particular scene, Harry's stress has been building after his divorce, and when he runs into his ex-wife at the store with her new husband, he finally snaps. Sally, having her own issues with her ex-boyfriend who has married someone else, retaliates. Here's the critical point: After Sally says her last word, Harry asks, "Are you finished?" Sally, trying to contain her emotions, simply says yes. Harry hugs her and says how sorry he is.

When we lose our temper, we hurt those we love. Children are especially sensitive to anger. They often don't understand where it is coming from, so they will assume it is something they did. Even adults are affected by negative outbursts. It has been said that a harsh, mean word will require more than ten kind words to overcome the trauma! Our tongues can truly be weapons, and all of us need to work harder at watching what we say and how we let off steam.

Anger is only one letter short of danger.

—UNKNOWN

Play Hard

I exercise to burn off stress. On one particular day, I was steaming. I showed up to teach my evening spin class, full of pent-up frustration and anger. After the hour was over, I looked at the class, and everyone was barely able to stand, leaning on their bikes in exhaustion. They asked, "What got into you?" I now warn them when I have extra stress to burn! But, hey, I felt better afterwards.

How do *you* work off stress? Don't forgo it, ever. Otherwise, tension will build up and rear its ugly head. Playing hard and doing the things you love can really reduce that buildup. In the spaces below, make a list of things you enjoy so you'll have options to consider when you really need them.

My Stress Busters

_____ _____

_____ _____

_____ _____

_____ _____

_____ _____

_____ _____

One of the suggestions I offered to a couple who were training with me was boxing pads and gloves. They loved the concept of working out together in this way. One day, they showed up at my studio with words of advice: don't box when you are mad at each other! They *really* took it out on each other. They laughed and admitted that they had eventually worked through their tension so that they could actually *talk*.

Keep Swinging

In tennis and in life, double faults happen. We can practice and play, but we are still human. Errors will happen. I believe that is what attracts people to watching sports. Sure, they are professionals, but they are human. They have bad days too. Nothing is guaranteed.

Play enough tennis, and you will get hit by a tennis ball. I have lost track of all the times opponents have hit me. At the time, it sure stings. One time during doubles, a friend on the opposite court was supposed to be serving to my partner, but he mishit the ball right into my leg. I had a bruise the size of a small cantaloupe for weeks!

These things happen, and in time we move on. We will make mistakes, and life may beat us down when we don't deserve it. Don't get sucked into the black hole of misery. Allowing yourself to feel bad for one day is OK, but letting it go on and on without changing it or getting help isn't. You deserve better!

The best way to recover from double faults is to keep swinging. Never give up! I love the saying:

*Go over, go around, go under or go through, but
never ever give up!*

Don't Forget

I find great peace in knowing that ultimately I'm not in charge. God is in control. When I mess up, God's plans will prevail—they may just take a little longer. The same is true for you, my friend. If you have been living a life out of control, God is ready to help you create order. Take the steps. Do it. Be it!

Conclusion

Today Is the Beginning of the Rest of Your Life

Be of good cheer. Do not think of today's failures, but of the successes that may come tomorrow. You have set yourselves a difficult task, but you will succeed if you persevere; and you will find a joy in overcoming obstacles. Remember, no effort that we make to attain something beautiful is ever lost.

—HELEN KELLER

 Do you ever struggle with feelings of failure? Do you look back with regrets? Do you feel you are unworthy of God's love? I know of a woman who lost a young child in an accident and blames herself. She believes God couldn't possibly love her since she let this happen. The rest of her life has been spent feeling sick and trying to find the cause through countless doctors when, in reality, she is physically healthy. Spiritually she is not. She hasn't settled her grief, pain, and sorrow with God. She will forever stay unbalanced until she lets go and forgives herself. Matters such as these are never easy, but God wants us whole. He knows our pain and suffering. He is the ultimate comforter!

Fear can prevent us from moving ahead. We must have the courage to take that next step. After all, tomorrow is another day. One of the greatest challenges people face in losing weight, for instance, is sticking with it. When they have a bad day and fall off the wagon, they feel they have failed and may give up. The vicious cycle continues: low self-esteem, weight gain, poor health, and lagging energy. To break the cycle, we need to get it through our heads that God has already forgotten yesterday! Tomorrow is a fresh start. Period.

Whether you slipped up on your diet, haven't forgiven yourself, or took back a problem you relinquished to God, you can start anew tomorrow. Don't beat yourself up over what is already done. Oh, the energy we waste on reliving the past. I'm guilty. Up until eight years ago, I rehashed every broken relationship I ever had in order to determine what I did wrong. I replayed my failures and bad judgments over and over again in my head. I felt like an utter flop. This is not healthy, and it certainly isn't how God sees us! I have made improvements on my stress management through the years, but this was one that hung on longer. It has taken several life traumas to get my attention.

I don't know if you are like that—you need to be hit over the head with a frying pan to get it? I hope not, but many of us can be stubborn. Ever see the classic movie *Monty Python and the Holy Grail*? In one scene, a knight gets his arms and legs cut off one by one, but he is still willing to fight, saying, "It's just a flesh wound." That is the stubborn person's mantra! Lord, help us.

In my own case, I finally realized what I was doing and decided to change. I believe you are doing the same, and I commend you! Thank you again for reading this book. Buy it for others. My prayer is that it will have a positive impact on your life and on others as well.

I encourage you to stick with your journey because, like my friend's onion, you *will* have layers. Under each issue lies another. Don't be discouraged by this; instead, see the upside—you are healing and improving, layer by layer, day by day.

The thing always happens that you really believe in; and the belief in a thing makes it happen.

—FRANK LLOYD WRIGHT

Believe

I know of two women who came from very similar situations. They both had dysfunctional, unhealthy families and were raped when they were younger. How they handled it, though, was quite different. One ignored her pain, suppressing it deep within her. She acted out her anger by being promiscuous and wild. She got into stripping, married and divorced numerous times, and had an abortion. To this day, in her forties, she is still running from her past. She is miserable and has alienated her good friends because of her continued drama. She is no further along the journey, repeating mistakes over and over again; she is stuck.

By contrast, the other woman chose to look her pain squarely in the eye. She went into counseling, sought God with a vengeance, and dealt with her pain. It was not easy, and talk about layers! Through some of them, she got depressed, anxious, and ill, but she persisted. Today, in her forties, she is happily married with wonderful children.

Whatever your past looks like, do not let it determine your tomorrow. You are not what you did years ago. You *can* live a different life.

You are not what you did years ago.

If you get anything out of this book, know that you can have more peace and balance in your life. You can create a new and improved you. Little steps will get you there! You are a creation of God and are in the process of growing and developing into an amazing person with an awesome life.

Make Every Day Count

Life is short. Just recently, the man I described previously in this book as my mentor, who twenty-eight years ago became like a father to me, was diagnosed with a terminal brain tumor. The news hit me like a ton of bricks, and I was faced with a wave of emotions. Both my real parents died of cancer, so at first I was very angry. I couldn't believe it was happening to me again. After hearing the news, I gave myself permission to be selfish and whine for an entire day: "Poor me." "Why is this happening to me?" Blah, blah, blah. Although the emotions were real, I knew they would not help the situation long-term. But I knew I needed to feel them. Once I regained my composure, I turned my attention toward what I could do to help. Living a long distance away, I picked up the phone as often as I could, but more important I prayed. I prayed specifically, diligently, and relentlessly. This became my priority. He had spent fifty years in ministry serving others; his life was too valuable to be snuffed out. I wasn't going to give up even though he had an awful outlook.

Just because you are reading a book on how to get your life back doesn't mean life will cooperate. Just because I wrote a book on managing your life doesn't mean I'm guaranteed smooth sailing. In fact, sometimes it seems just the opposite. As I mentioned earlier, when someone commits to losing weight, events rise up to prevent it. Or when a person decides to simplify her life, a family member will need to move in for assistance. Life doesn't give any of us a break. And none of us get out of here alive.

When we embark on major changes that will have a huge positive impact on others and ourselves, be prepared for resistance. Every time I write a book, I brace myself. I can expect challenges in the very areas I am writing on. Situations will arise that force me to practice what I preach. I consider it more material! I am in process, and so are you. When life hits you, fight back! This is your life; use your tools and the power God has given you.

When life hits you, fight back!

In the case of my adopted dad and his brain tumor, prayer and faith were our tools. Among all his family members, we recruited thousands and thousands of friends and church members across the globe to pray. We also believed without doubt that he would be cured. I deliberately had to erase my fears and thoughts of possible death. I wasn't in denial but in true obedience to God's promises and trusted him with every ounce of my being for deliverance. Although my dad was given only three months to live, he is still alive. God provided a miracle! The lessons we all learned:

1. God is all-powerful
2. God is still the Great Healer
3. God is in control
4. God is bigger than all our problems
5. Prayer works
6. Life is short—live it like there is no tomorrow

I know all too well that things don't always turn out this happily. After all, both my parents are gone already. But we must continue to have faith, believe, and trust God. And because life is so short, we need to live it to the fullest.

Seize the Day

I know we have heaven to look toward. In my dad's case, he was OK with dying if that was God's will, but he didn't want to hurt his loved ones left behind. He is now enjoying God-given time with his family and making the most of every minute. He is seizing the day, and we should all do the same.

Carpe diem!

Seize every moment you are given. We are not promised or guaranteed tomorrow, but we do have these moments right here and now. We can spend them whining and complaining, becoming a victim like so many women I see. They blame their parents, husbands, and society for their problems because it is easier than looking in the mirror and admitting their part. Choosing to be a victim will only keep you in the dark and prevent you from experiencing God's light. Nothing in your life will change for the better; it will only get worse. Instead, choose to be joyful. I'm not suggesting that we ignore negative feelings; we are humans with emotions, and we need to feel them. Just be sure you don't get stuck in any one negative emotion for too long.

A friend of mine was coming to visit one day, and she woke up in a funk. She really didn't feel like getting ready to come exercise with me, but she decided to "lock her funk in her car trunk" and drove over anyway. We had a really fun workout together, and her spirits were lifted. When she opened her trunk back up, her funk was gone. Apparently it smothered to death! Don't let negative emotions prevent you from experiencing all God has for you, and he has a world full!

What poison is to food, self-pity is to life.

—OLIVER C. WILSON

Stay on the Path

The world isn't going to change just because we are trying so very hard to improve. The reality is that the world may actually seem harsher, faster, and more out of control to you once you regain some sense of order. We can never get rid of stress completely. What we can do, though, is respond to it in healthier ways. That is really the purpose of this book—to equip you with alternative ways of coping with life. We have all tried the other ways, and they simply don't work long-term. Food won't comfort you; it will only make you gain weight. Alcohol won't make the pain go away; it will only numb your senses, making it easier for you to make additional mistakes. Smoking won't really take your mind off your troubles; it will only deprive you of oxygen so you can't think straight. Avoiding pain doesn't make it go away; it makes it ten times bigger and more stressful. Whatever unhealthy way you have used in the past to manage your stress is only adding to the problem.

You've started on a new path; stay on it. I love the Christmas cartoon *Santa Claus Is Coming to Town*. In it, Chris Kringle sings, "Put one foot in front of the other, and soon you'll be walking out the door." It's a cute song with a serious reminder for us that little steps, one by one, get us there.

> *Victory is won not in miles, but in inches. Win a little now, hold your ground, and later win a little more.*
> —Louis L'Amour

So often society pushes and almost demands immediate results. With microwave ovens, drive-through windows, and instant messaging, the world seems to be moving faster every day. People are losing the ability to slow down and understand that some things, important things, do take time. When I was going through my divorce, I had a "friend" tell me after two weeks that she had had enough. I was to call her when I was over this and would be more fun again. The world can be crazy sometimes. But just because we are in the world doesn't mean we have to be *of* the world. We can set our own pace. And I believe we are called to.

Lead the Way

If we don't show an example of a better way, who will? Our children need to know that another way exists, and the best way to ensure that is to show them. As you develop a new life that is more balanced, share your experiences with others. If you find something in this book to be helpful, pass it on.

While you're leading, slow down! Do you remember being a teenager waiting for a big dance or another event and saying to your parents, "Oh, I'm so bored! Time is going too slowly"? I think every parent has told a child, "Just wait until you are older. Time will fly by so fast your head will spin." Boy, they weren't kidding. The weeks go faster and the months click away in a flash. The more you can bring control back and slow your life down, the more enjoyable it will be. You won't feel like you are missing out or watching from the outside; you will be *in* your life. You will have more of a say in what you do with your time. You will be creating the life *you* want. And you will have even more time to learn and grow.

Keep Learning

Education is learning what you didn't even know you didn't know.

—DANIEL BOORSTIN

I know I'm still learning. All of us are. You will have your own experiences to share with others. Every day presents new situations and opportunities. What worked in one situation may not work for another, so we will constantly be applying and learning new ways to manage stress. Life is constantly changing, and so are people. How we handle a person one time may not work the next time because they too are on a journey. As the cartoon says, "Just when I figured out all the answers, they changed the questions!"

Learning is an adventure. When we stop learning, we die.

Trust God

Who we become is determined both by the choices we make and by God's hand in our lives. When we are wondering where in the world God is and why he isn't fixing something, he is usually waiting for us to take action. When we do, he is right there beside us, helping us get through. He knows our circumstances and who we can become, because he is the one who created us. He has faith in us. We must trust him.

When you create new habits, patterns, thoughts, and beliefs, have faith that God will assist you. As the saying goes, if we see only one set of footprints in the sand, it is because God is carrying us. When you get weary on your journey—and you will— lean on him. When you are troubled that the trip isn't going as you planned, pray for peace. All along, know that God is on your side. So am I. We're rooting for you and cheering you on as you make your way to the *you* that you were destined to be.

Take your life back, my friend! Live it, love it, and be in it. I wish you my heart's best and God's rich blessings.

Jabez cried out to the God of Israel, "Oh, that you would bless me and enlarge my territory! Let your hand be with me, and keep me from harm so that I will be free from pain." And God granted his request.

—1 Chronicles 4:10

Bibliography

Allen, James. *As a Man Thinketh*. New York: Barnes & Noble, 1992.

Bossé-Smith, Lorraine. *A Healthier, Happier You: 101 Steps for Lessening Stress*. Uhrichsville, Ohio: Barbour, 2003.

Bossé-Smith, Lorraine and John Jackson. *Leveraging Your Leadership Style*. Nashville: Abingdon Press, 2007.

Chapman, Gary. *The Five Love Languages*. Chicago: Northfield, 1995.

Cloud, Henry and John Townsend. *Boundaries*. Grand Rapids: Zondervan, 1992.

Cook, John. *The Book of Positive Quotations*. Minneapolis: Rubicon Press, Inc., 1993.

Covey, Stephen R. *First Things First*. New York: Simon & Schuster, 1994.

Gallwey, W. Timothy. *The Inner Game of Tennis*. New York: Random House, 1997.

Lencioni, Patrick. *The Five Dysfunctions of a Team*. San Francisco: Jossey-Bass, 2002.

Smith, Steve and Lorraine Smith. *Mastering Time Management*. Murrieta, Calif.: Concept One, 2001.

————. *Overcoming Time Traps.* Murrieta, Calif.: Concept One, 2002.

————. *Time to Manage!* Murrieta, Calif.: Concept One, 1991.

Swenson, Richard A. *Margin.* Colorado Springs, Colo.: Nav-Press, 1992.

van Ekern, Glenn. *The Speaker's Sourcebook II.* Englewood Cliffs, N.J.: Prentice Hall, 1994.

Worley, Karla. *Growing Weary Doing Good?* Birmingham: New Hope Publishers, 2001.